T0356801

THE BARNES MUSEUM AND HOMESTEAD

CHRISTINA VOLPE

Foreword by Phil Wooding, Southington Town Historian

THE
History
PRESS

Published by The History Press
Charleston, SC
www.historypress.com

First published 2025

Manufactured in the United States

ISBN 9781467158428

Library of Congress Control Number: 2024949863

To my Nonno Attillio, who brought our family to Southington.
Thank you for building a life for us here.

And to my daughter, AnnaMaria, and all the children growing up in Southington
just like I did—may we always stay curious.
And remember: history is all around us—we just have to look.

CONTENTS

Foreword, by Phil Wooding, Southington Town Historian 7
Preface 11
Acknowledgements 13

1. The Roots of Southington 15
2. Foundations of Fortune 26
3. The Victorian Era in Southington 43
4. From Heir to Heirloom: Barnes Inheritance 60
5. Echoes of the Civil War 75
6. Bradley Barnes, Southington's Richest Man 90
7. A Legacy in Glass 100
8. The Bequeathal and Its Impact 109

Notes 119
Bibliography 121
About the Author 127

FOREWORD

Bradley Henry Barnes was born in 1883, and my father, Milton Johnson Wooding, was born in 1911. Neither gentleman would have imagined that in 1973, my father would be in the Bradley and Barnes Homestead with the charge of trying to make it into a museum. Bradley died in 1973, and his wife, Leila Upson, had predeceased him by twenty-one years. The couple was childless and had few close relatives. They lived in the home together on North Main Street for forty-three years. A personal diary entry by Bradley indicated that he felt a tremendous loss at his wife's passing in 1953, writing in his journal, "My all gone forever."

Bradley remained in the home and led a very quiet existence until his passing nearly twenty years after his wife. I believe it can be said that Bradley and Leila led a comfortable but not ostentatious life to the casual observer. In fact, it was not until reading his twenty-eight-page will that it was realized how wealthy he was, as well as how generous he was to many charitable organizations and institutions in Southington and throughout Connecticut. Among the disbursements in his will was $6 million to Bradley Memorial Hospital of Southington, initially endowed by his aunt, Julia Arnold Bradley, in 1919. Bradley Barnes's 1973 will also left the Barnes Homestead and all of its furnishing to the Town of Southington on the condition that it be maintained by the town's Library Board of Directors, primarily as a historical library and museum. If the town declined to accept the bequest, the home and contents would be returned to the estate. What was perceived by many as a grand gesture to the town soon became an unwanted gift, as the town leaders responsible for making the "yes" or "no" decision held up the transfer of the home for some time. Town residents who favored receiving the home wrote letters to town officials and local newspapers advocating for Bradley's gift. When approval was finally obtained, it fell to the library board to start the process of having someone take on Bradley's wishes to turn his home into a museum.

My father, Milton, had recently retired from almost forty years at the local Peck Stow & Wilcox Company and had been a Library Board of Directors member for many years. He was chairman of the board and became chairman of the Building Committee for the new library, which was completed in 1974. He also had a deep interest in town history and had the business mind for organization. He volunteered to take on the job of assessing the home and reporting back to the library board regularly. On May 10, 1979, he wrote, "The Southington Public Library Board appointed me Executive Director of the Barnes Museum, 85 North Main St., Southington, CT in November 1973. Since that time, I have been completely immersed in the almost overwhelming amount of documentation covering the day-to-day events in the lives of three generations of members of one family, as recorded in over fifty diaries and thousands of letters. These documents not only reveal daily activities but also provide a nineteenth-century sociological and historical record of the town of Southington."

People who stopped in to see how Dad was doing left with the observation that the goal was probably unattainable. Fortunately, Dad had the positive attitude to say often, "You eat an elephant one bite at a time." He had some help too. My mother, Helen Karl Wooding, had recently retired and also became a "member of the Barnes Family." Considering the home was completely furnished and left as it was after Bradley passed, it is not a great leap to feel a sense of "belonging" to the house. It was not long before I felt compelled to assist, even though I was still working. The Wooding family cleaned, moved and sorted material in preparation for the house to become a museum and open to the public. Dad was the master of understatement and, on one occasion, asked us to start washing a few of the glass goblets in the collection. At some point in their lives, both Bradley and Leila had decided to collect goblets. Dad started delivering boxes of goblets to us in the Barnes kitchen as mom and I started the washing and drying process. After doing about two hundred or so pieces, we thought for sure we were near the end of the collection. Mom made the query as to how many more there were, and Dad, very quietly, said, "About a thousand more." On another occasion, Dad asked me to assist him in moving "some magazines" to the attic. When

I got to the attic, I realized that Bradley had saved about every issue of every magazine relating to things he was interested in, especially cars, radios and horses. These interests remain apparent throughout his home today. In another instance, the local fire marshal directed that the large amount of coal remaining in the cellar should be removed. A few friends and I had a firsthand historical experience shoveling coal well after when it had been the fuel of choice for heating for more than a century. Afterward, we all looked like coal miners, but somehow I still had a few friends after that.

The Bradley Barnes home cannot be described as the house of a hoarder, as some have said in the past, but it is more of an extensive collection kept for posterity in a semblance of order. As time went by, Dad became more convinced that Bradley and his ancestors had either willingly or unintentionally planned for the home to become a storehouse of their family's history. The three of us Woodings started giving tours of the house, now designated as the Barnes Museum, by private appointment to a few members of the community in November 1974. We used 3x5 index cards with whatever information was available at the time about the many antiquities found throughout the house. Eventually, the 3x5 cards were replaced with sheets of paper that contained more detailed information gleaned from continuous research into the Barnes family diaries, letters and invoices saved from purchases over the years. The activity at Barnes became known to newspapers, and many sought Milton for interviews and photos of progress toward the opening for the general public. Increasingly, people sought out the historical information that was and continues to be available at the museum. With the advent of computers, social media and cellphones, any reference to "history" often happens in the last fifteen minutes. The much longer timeline has faded to the point of relevance. Time becomes much more of the present than of the previous. The Barnes Museum is an example of the opposite, where the home pushes aside the present and instead shows a totally different era, with a way of life passed down through three generations. The house has been a compendium of economic and social activity for the past 188 years. The evolution of our nation's history is evident, as technological improvements are visible from the building of the house in 1836 to the time of Bradley's passing in 1973. The museum has also evolved to include programs outside the grounds and home, with many events bringing people inside the museum.

I am sure that Dad would be especially pleased that the museum has rightfully continued to expand its programming to attract both local guests and people from far beyond Southington. He would be most grateful and appreciative that the "unwanted gift" has proven to be the gift that keeps on giving. In 2024, as I mark fifty years of volunteering at the Barnes and my wife marks forty-five years since joining the Wooding trio here, we have witnessed the home's transformation into a museum of note, as evidenced by the many events and programs being offered throughout the year. We realize that we do not preserve history for our grandparents but for our grandchildren. Enjoy this wonderfully detailed history of the Barnes family of Southington and their home turned museum, as presented by the current curator, Christina Volpe, in this book. She has quickly become another treasured member of the Barnes family.

—PHIL WOODING, Southington Town Historian

PREFACE

For years, the legacy of Bradley Barnes and the significance of the Barnes Museum have been somewhat misunderstood. Sometimes dismissed as a "hoarder house" because of its overwhelming collection of artifacts, the museum was frequently overlooked by residents—many of whom could vaguely recall visiting once but couldn't quite remember when. The museum's true value, hidden beneath layers of collected history, remains a hidden gem in our community and in the state of Connecticut. Among all the stories and relics relating to the late Bradley Barnes families, one poignant detail has quietly faded into the background: the tragic death of Bradley's mother, Alice, who passed away when her son was fourteen. This loss profoundly shaped Bradley's life and, in turn, influenced the history preserved within these walls. The fact that Alice's story has been so often overlooked speaks volumes about how collective memory, the way we remember history as a community, is shaped—and how easily it can be skewed by the narratives we choose to remember.

The reality of Bradley's life is recorded in diaries and personal artifacts scattered throughout the museum, each telling its own story. Everything at the Barnes Museum is original, from the intricate leaded glass to the worn wooden floors. The collection spans from the late 1700s through the 1970s and includes everything from the earliest land deeds recorded in town to an East Asian dish dating to the 1500s. Objects that are not original are identified on our tours, but the overwhelming majority of what you see here is as it was, a living snapshot of the family's history. To really understand Bradley's life, we encourage visitors to think about the grandeur of Newport's Gilded Age mansions, built by families like the Vanderbilts, Astors and Morgans. These families amassed enormous fortunes, reshaping entire industries and leaving behind a legacy of wealth that spread far beyond their communities. For example, Cornelius Vanderbilt II built The Breakers in Newport with a fortune that would be counted in the billions today. Bradley's fortune, while significant, was more modest in comparison, valued at an approximate $20 million today. He was part of the regional elite whose influence was deeply felt in Southington, although it didn't reach the grandiosity of the Newport crowd. But in his own way, Bradley was doing the same thing those businessmen were doing in Newport, just on a local scale. His investments in real estate, local manufacturing and trade were strategic and industrious; his summer home was a small cottage on the coast in Guilford. Bradley's life was one that reflected solid, comfortable influence rather than flashy, ostentatious wealth. In Southington during its more formidable years between 1830 and 1900, Bradley's grandfather Amon Bradley laid the groundwork for the family's generational success by becoming a leading figure in town, leaving for his grandson a legacy rooted in community and family, not in national empire-building. This is Southington's own version of the Gilded Age, with the Barnes Museum at its heart.

Over the last fifty years since the Barnes Museum became a part of the town, some of this history has faded from collective memory, but my hope is that you take away from this book the knowledge that you don't have to visit the museum to learn about the Bradley and Barnes families. Their legacy is present in every corner of this community. From the architecture that lines Main Street to the fountains on the Town Green and in Plantsville that honor them, this family's history is woven into the fabric of Southington. This book aims to bring those stories back to the forefront, reminding us all of the rich history that surrounds us—history that has shaped not just the museum but the town itself. As we walk these streets, live in these homes and build our own lives here, we continue to carry forward the legacy of those who came before us. This book is a way to honor that legacy, to hopefully keep it alive and to ensure that future generations understand and appreciate the deep roots that have made Southington what it is today.

ACKNOWLEDGEMENTS

I would like to begin by expressing my deepest gratitude to the Town of Southington and its dedicated staff, whose unwavering commitment to this community and the collective effort required to keep the Barnes Museum running smoothly have made this project possible. I am profoundly thankful for the support of former Town Manager Mark Sciota, current Town Manager Alex Ricciardone, Finance Director Jim Bowes and Assistant Finance Director Christina Sivigny-Smith. Their encouragement breathed life into this project, and their ongoing support of the Barnes Museum's operations ensures that this treasured place remains as beautiful and vibrant as ever, both inside and out. I must also extend my heartfelt thanks to Southington Public Library Executive Director Thomas Piezzo, whose encouragement during the writing stage was not only helpful but essential. His insights and mentorship were invaluable, guiding me through this journey with wisdom and kindness. I cannot thank him enough for the role he played in shaping this work. In addition to this team, thank you to the dedicated Board of the Southington Public Library and Barnes Museum, especially Tina, Missy, and Peter—thank you for believing in me and this work.

A special acknowledgment is due to Outreach Coordinator and Preservationist of the Barnes Museum Nadia Dillon, although she is so much more than that to me. Nadia's passion for and dedication to caring for the collection match, if not surpass, my own. Without her to bounce ideas off of, share the inevitable frustrations and meticulously gather photos, I'm not sure how this project would have come together. Her deep knowledge of Alice Bradley and her diligent work in compiling Alice's life into archival folders provided the foundation for much of the information about Alice in this book. Nadia, this work is as much yours as it is mine.

I would be remiss not to acknowledge all those who came before me and played an incredible role as stewards of the museum. I especially want to thank the curator who preceded me, Marie Secondo, who, along with Bonnie Plourde, dedicated more than fifteen years to caring for the museum. Their research, countless hours of dedication and meticulous attention to the homestead and its collection have made this book possible in so many ways. To Liz and Mark Kopec for sharing so much of their knowledge and collection of Southington ephemera with me. To Phil Wooding and the Southington Historical Society, I am eternally grateful for your assistance in providing records, memories, photographs and so much more. Phil, you welcomed me into the museum with open arms, and you have become my favorite research buddy, always ready to nerd out over Southington history. Without you and your wonderful wife, Brenda, this job would be infinitely more challenging. Brenda, along with the Friends of the Barnes—Chris, Alison, Barbara and Heidi—thank you for believing in this museum, for volunteering your time and for trusting in my sometimes wild ideas. Your dedication is the true spirit of this place. I would like to also thank all the volunteers and interns who have worked with me during my time here. It has been a profound privilege to work with each of you and watch your passion for history grow. You all are the reason I do this work—to keep these stories alive and pass them down.

Thank you to my family, especially my fiancé, Tevin, my Corinthian column, holding me up both literally and figuratively throughout this process. I cannot wait to marry you. To my daughter, Anna, thank you for being my best curatorial assistant—this career of mine has grown with you, and I could not be more blessed to have you by my side in whatever archive I find myself in. To my TT, the Mom of all Moms, I would not be who I am today without your love and support. Thank you for giving me antiquities, art, curiosity and passion.

Finally, to my former professors in the History Department at Central Connecticut State University, especially Dr. Warshauer and Dr. Glaser, I feel I forever owe you both a debt of gratitude. You changed my life for the better and equipped me with the skills, tools and resources to do this work. Thank you for teaching me to appreciate place. It is because of you that I seek out history and strive to preserve it, and for that, I will be forever grateful.

CHAPTER 1

THE ROOTS OF SOUTHINGTON

THE EARLY AGRICULTURAL COMMUNITY

The cultivation of the earth is the most important labor of man. When tillage begins, other arts follow. The farmers, therefore, are the founders of human civilization.

—Daniel Webster

The area now known as Southington was originally occupied by the Tunxis and Quinnipiac tribes, Indigenous Algonquian-speaking peoples who used the region for hunting, fishing and seasonal migrations. Conflict over land use and rights between Indigenous peoples and European colonists erupted in the 1630s in the form of the Pequot War, which prompted many English colonists to migrate southward from where they landed in Massachusetts to seek new territories, moving into the fertile Connecticut River Valley. The land that became Southington is nestled in a valley between Ragged Mountain to the east and the western ridge of the Metacomet Ridge, which includes the notable peaks of Bradley Mountain and Short Mountain. The valley stretches out in meadows perfect for farming, wetlands rich from the Quinnipiac River and shaded forests steeping with game. These lands were initially claimed by early settlers as part of greater Farmington and are commonly referred to as the "South Meadow" or "South Farmington." By 1698, the area's rocky soil, while challenging for farming, proved attractive enough for settlers seeking new opportunities.

Residents of this new settlement—unable to return daily to Farmington for goods, services and worship—sought to establish their own meetinghouse. By 1721, South Farmington residents had petitioned for winter privileges to have a preacher minister locally, reflecting their growing independence and community spirit. By 1726, the area was referred to as the South Society of Farmington, and a meetinghouse was allowed to be erected for independent meetings and worship. This marked a significant step toward the development of an autonomous Southington, a town that would grow steadily despite the challenges of its rocky, swampy terrain.

In 1760, certain inhabitants of South Farmington living on Wolcott Mountain, along with those from neighboring Waterbury, petitioned the General Assembly for distinct society privileges. The petition, signed by twenty-four leading residents, faced opposition and was initially rejected. Key figures such as Jonathan Root from Southington and Thomas Clark and Phineas Roys from Waterbury were called to justify their request.[1] Despite repeated rejections, a petition in September 1762 successfully secured the right to have a preacher in the community for five months and the establishment of a school. The question of separating the South Farmington community continued to face resistance from Farmington and Waterbury, leading to multiple memorials and counter-memorials being presented to the General Assembly. Committees were appointed to investigate, including one in 1764 that reported against granting the privileges. Another committee in 1770 finally reported favorably. As a result, the General Assembly granted society privileges and rights to the South Farmington inhabitants, officially naming it Farmingbury. In October 1779, Southington was incorporated as a separate town.

What did Southington look like in 1800? It was a small, rural community with a population of fewer than one thousand residents. The town's landscape was characterized by its rolling hills and farmland, with mountains as a backdrop to daily duties, commutes and activities. Each resident lived on a family-owned farm, with homes scattered across the countryside. The town's makeup was modest, featuring a few essential buildings such as the meetinghouse, a school and a handful of shops and taverns that catered to everyday living and survival. Dirt roads connected the farms and the town center, often lined with stone walls built from the rocky soil. The community was close-knit, with neighbors relying on one another for trade, labor, safety and socializing, especially during planting and harvest seasons. The overall atmosphere in Southington was one that we would describe today as simplicity and self-sufficiency, reflecting the hardworking spirit of the

View from Southington of the Hanging Hills of Meriden.

early settlers. It is in this early agrarian atmosphere that Amon Bradley, the defining character of the book you're about to read, was born. The farmhand turned future philanthropist, industrialist and banker was born in a time in American history marked by the War of 1812, a conflict that tested the resilience of the young nation and influenced its economic and political landscape. Amid the backdrop of rural Southington, Amon Bradley's early life would have been shaped by the community's agrarian lifestyle, evolving industrial progress and experimentation and the patriotic pride that defined the early nineteenth century.

AMON BRADLEY:
THE MAKING OF A YANKEE PEDDLER

Amon Bradley was born in 1812, the youngest of eight children. At the time of his birth, there was only one economy in America and that was the agricultural economy. To support a large family and their family's farming business, colonial traditions and law provided certain protections to the head of the household, usually the father, to help the family thrive on their land. Amon Bradley learned from his father the business of the family farm and how to take care of himself and his family through and by the land. He tilled soil each summer, harvested in the fall, gathered ice with his siblings from Bradley Lake in the winter and worked the land that is now known as Crescent Lake, a public park in Southington.

Amon Bradley's father, Ichabod, was born on November 10, 1784, in East Haven, Connecticut. His father, Daniel Bradley, was thirty-nine, and his mother, Sarah, was thirty-five. Sarah died following Ichabod's birth. Daniel and his son, Ichabod, came to Southington from East Haven in 1779 when he was fifteen years old. Daniel had inherited a significant amount of land in Southington, including a lake and surrounding mountain from his first wife Sarah Judd's grandfather Benjamin Judd, who received the property from King George himself.[2] Initially, the family lived nearby on what is contemporary Andrews Street in Southington but eventually worked to build their humble home beside the lake. On November 27, 1788, at the age of twenty-four, Ichabod married his second wife, Abigail Moore Bradley, in Southington, where together they had eight children over twenty-two years of their early marriage. He continued to build on his land inheritance, but it required work, as it was overgrown marshland beside the lake. The initial property Ichabod cleared included the abutting lake and all of Bradley Mountain, which stretched from Southington into the nearby town of Plainville—nearly two hundred acres. Many of the rock walls that you encounter today when hiking or walking through the trails at present-day Crescent Lake were built by Ichabod and his sons. Ichabod was married to Abigail for more than forty years. She died in early 1832, and he held on for six months before his passing on October 13, 1832, at the age of sixty-seven. Initially, the couple were interred on their farm, but they were later removed and interred within the Bradley family plot at Oak Hill Cemetery. Their children were Polly (born 1789), Wyllys (born 1791), Roswell (born 1794), William (born 1798), Diademia (born 1801), Hiel (born 1804), Charles (born 1808) and Amon (born 1812).[3]

It is here beside the lake and next to the mountain where Amon Bradley grew up, working hard to maintain and sustain life in colonial America. When the farm could afford to lose his help, he attended the local school and the village academy. As a child, his interests were in the bartering and trading of goods and in reading legal books, something that would carry into his adult life. Life on the Bradley farm required work, and that work determined a family's economic and social standing within the community.

William Tolman Carlton, the Yankee Peddler. *Harvard Art Museum, collections online, April 2, 2024, https://hvrd.art/o/231947.*

Bradley Mountain Farm, circa 1870.

The men often carried the responsibility for the majority of agricultural labor, including clearing trees and constructing structures like barns and outhouses. It was a time of single-minded determination and hands-on survival. Women were producers of goods that were derived from the raw materials that were provided by the labor of the farm, turning such things into clothing, food and numerous other items for daily living. Until the commercial production of textiles in New England, home spinning was an important and ongoing task. In the 1830s, many garments were created from either the fields, flax or sheep's wool. Neither of these tasks were simple in terms of labor spent to produce the goods, be it farming or homemaking. Wool production required cleaning, carding, spinning and eventually weaving, all of which required skill and took place before a single stitch could be formed. Farmhands, or Amon's siblings, also took part in butchering, cleaning, hanging and cutting their own meats, some of which they raised on the farm and others they hunted in near the lake or on Bradley Mountain. Making butter, cheese, liquor, soaps and candles all on the homestead were all customary in the early 1800s, and each task required a great deal of labor.

When Ichabod died in 1832, the farm was inherited by his elder sons, William and Hiel. Ichabod was a man characterized by his thriftiness, perseverance and integrity. These characteristics were passed on to his sons and daughters. In Ichabod Bradley's will, Amon Bradley was bequeathed a significant portion of his father's estate. Specifically, Amon received the remaining undivided fourth part of the land and buildings, ensuring him a substantial share of the family property. Additionally, he was granted an equal share of all the rest of Ichabod's estate, both real and personal, which was to be divided equally among Amon and his brothers. This inheritance marked a notable contribution to Amon's assets and laid the foundation for his future prospects—if he was wise about his investments.

Amon Bradley was just twenty years old when his father died. As a young man, Amon Bradley was entering a rapidly evolving American landscape deeply intertwined with the state's own unique history and dynamics. Connecticut, known as the "Constitution State," played a pivotal role in the nation's early development, with a rich legacy of innovation, commerce and social reform. By the mid-1800s, Connecticut was at the forefront of industrialization, particularly in cities like Hartford and New Haven, where manufacturing flourished, fueled by abundant access to waterways and a growing, diversely skilled workforce. In 1790, the Patent Office was established, and soon after, Eli Whitney, one of Connecticut's most notable figures, established a firearm manufacturing facility in New Haven in 1798. Whitney revolutionized the industry by pioneering the use of interchangeable parts in firearm production, which elevated Connecticut's reputation in the industry.[4] Gradually during the early nineteenth century, Connecticut's manufacturing sector became prominent in textiles, firearms, machinery and much more—enough to drive significant economic growth and urbanization out of the city centers and into the rural landscapes of communities like Southington. However, this transformative period posed its own challenges. While industrialization brought prosperity to some, it also exacerbated societal disparities, with working conditions often harsh and opportunities unevenly distributed.[5] Moreover, Connecticut, like the rest of the nation, grappled with the contentious issue of enslavement as debates over its expansion into new territories intensified.[6]

Amon Bradley's young adult life unfolded amid this early industrial boom. Within the geographical area of Southington, clockmaking and tin-smithing prospered. Eli Terry received his patent for an improved shelf clock mechanism on November 17, 1816. This patent was significant as it revolutionized clock manufacturing, making clocks more affordable and accessible to the public. In the 1820s and 1830s, Southington boasted several clockmaking shops. Clockmakers in the area were often carpenters or cabinetmakers who purchased the mechanisms after crafting the wooden cases.[7]

As Amon Bradley stepped outside the family farm for the first time following his father's death in 1832, in a bid for independence and financial stability, he made a daring choice to become a Yankee peddler. For Amon,

Teapot, circa 1835.

Left: *Southington Mirror*, June 9, 1865.

Right: Earliest photo of Sylvia Barnes Bradley found in the collection.

the decision wasn't just about making ends meet—it was about embracing a life of adventure and entrepreneurship in the budding years of a new nation. Using his portion of his father's estate to buy a peddlers cart, he set off with a modest collection of tin from Berlin and clocks from Southington.[8] As he set out on his journey with eyes toward the southern states, Amon saw himself as more than just a peddler; he pioneered commerce, navigating the ever-changing landscape of early nineteenth-century America. Armed with goods made on the family's farm, tin manufactured in nearby Berlin and Southington-made Yankee mantel clocks, he crisscrossed the countryside, trading wares and forging connections with customers in distant towns and villages.[9] For two years, Amon departed in the early fall with a wagon full of products and returned in the spring with enough money to settle any debts he may have incurred along his journey. By 1835, Amon had saved just enough money and made enough connections in the trading business to realize a new venture: opening his own mercantile business in his hometown of Southington. Returning to the quiet lakeside farm was no longer an option. This time he would make himself known by settling in the center of the community. His business was Amon Bradley & Company, located on the present-day Town Green on Main Street, providers of dry goods, tin, mantel clocks, textiles, medicine and more. Seemingly a man well-to-do, he was missing one thing: a family. Not long after his return to Southington, Amon began constructing a home less than a half mile from his store. This home would become the foundation for his family life, where he would enjoy sixty-seven years of marriage and the fondness of his three children. On October 9, 1836, Amon married Sylvia Barnes, one of the smartest moves he ever made.

Sylvia Barnes, born in Southington's Marion area in 1818, married Amon Bradley at the age of eighteen. When her father, Truman Barnes, died in August 1834, he left her $50 to complete her education and $500 from his estate to invest in real estate. This was a sizeable amount for a young unmarried woman in the 1830s (about $17,000 in 2024). Sylvia likely attended the Hartford Female Seminary, founded in 1823 by Catharine Beecher. This prestigious institution, located about twenty miles and a day's ride from Southington, offered a rigorous curriculum designed to provide young women with a good education that extended beyond their domestic duties. Sylvia's attendance at such an academy, and the encouragement she received from her father to continue attending, was progressive for the 1830s and indicates Truman Barnes's status as one of Southington's most prominent farmers. When Sylvia married Amon in 1836, she made Amon a long, beaded wedding chain, a popular gift made by young ladies in the 1830s. These chains were crafted on wooden looms with imported glass or bartered Native American beads. Sylvia's education equipped her with the knowledge and skills necessary to be a supportive

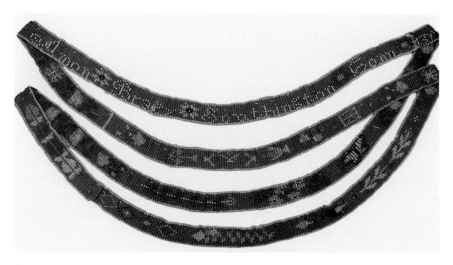

Beaded chain that Sylvia made for her husband as a wedding gift.

partner to Amon during those early years he was establishing his business and later as a supportive mother to their children.

Sylvia and Amon had three children. Their first was a son born in February 1843 named Franklin. Two more children followed: Alice in 1849 and Emma in 1857. Sylvia strongly encouraged each child to invest their time and efforts into their education, which laid a foundation for the family's success in both their personal and professional lives. Franklin graduated from Yale in 1863, while Alice had many musical recitals at nearby Lewis Academy. Emma received top marks and praise from her teachers, as is found in the museum's collection. Amon and Sylvia's partnership, built on mutual respect and shared goals, allowed them to use their wealth and love for their community to expand Amon's business practices and involvement in town commerce and politics. Amon and Sylvia's home, completed in 1836, was a Greek Revival house located on what was then known as the Cheshire Turnpike, today's 85 North Main Street. The then humble two-floor house featured two rooms on each floor and a central double-sided fireplace on the floor level. Upstairs was a bedroom facing the turnpike, with Amon's side of the bed near a window facing the direction of his shop on the Town Green. Behind their home, a detached summer kitchen in the rear served as Sylvia's domain, complete with a hearth for cooking, a space for canning and large sinks for washing. She was very much a woman of her time, cooking, cleaning and making the early American home what it has come to be known as in our collective memory.

In later chapters, we explore Sylvia's prowess over her household and the hard work that came with running the home of a successful businessman while simultaneously homesteading and raising three bright, spry children. Sylvia and Amon's partnership exemplified the blend of education, dedication and community philanthropy that defined their legacy in Southington. In 1847, Amon Bradley was appointed postmaster of Southington.[10] Throughout American history, the role of the postmaster has changed quite a bit. In early America, around the time Amon became postmaster, they played an essential role in expanding communication networks between villages and broadening access to the increasingly in-demand objects that were needed in the new American household: grain, molasses and more. Initially, local merchants or prominent citizens such as Amon often received and distributed mail from neighboring towns and villages. By the mid-nineteenth century, the postmaster had become a fixture in virtually every town and city across America, including rural Southington. In 1847, a typical day for Amon Bradley as postmaster would have been a whirlwind of activity as he sorted,

The early homestead was in the Greek Revival style.

stamped and distributed incoming and outgoing mail. It would have put him in contact with many of the town's citizens, and in the absence of a national bank, which wouldn't come until the National Banking Act of 1863, postage stamps served as a form of currency, hence postmasters played a significant role in selling and distributing stamps. The stamps served as payment for mail delivery and acted as small-denomination currency. People could buy stamps with cash and use them to pay for goods and services or exchange them for other forms of goods, services or other forms of currency. In this way, postmasters effectively acted as bankers, managing these transactions and providing those early vital financial services to their communities. Banker and financier were hats Amon would wear in the community in one way or another for many years to come. For a young farmer turned peddler turned merchant, Amon Bradley and his story are woven into the tapestry of the foundation of early America. His role may have been humble, but the impact of Amon Bradley receiving the trusted position of becoming postmaster for Southington in 1847 reverberated far beyond the walls of their home on North Main Street and is still felt beyond the walls of the Barnes Museum today.

CHAPTER 2

FOUNDATIONS OF FORTUNE

A s Amon Bradley's influence in Southington grew through his role as postmaster, his involvement in local business and his increasing real estate holdings, he began to look beyond his immediate family for support in his various ventures. In 1836, a pivotal moment came when Amon and Sylvia Bradley took in a young boy named Merrit Newell Woodruff. Merrit, who had lost his mother at a young age and whose father was struggling to rebuild a failed lumber business in New York, found a new home in Southington. For Amon and Sylvia, taking in Merrit was more than an act of charity—it was an investment in a young boy's future. Over time, Merrit would become an integral part of Amon's life, contributing to both the family's success and the growth of Southington itself.

THE INTRODUCTION OF MERRIT WOODRUFF:
A NEW CHAPTER IN AMON BRADLEY'S LIFE

Amon held the position of postmaster in Southington for twelve years, during which time his real estate properties, business ventures and political sway within Southington grew. Amon Bradley & Company, situated in the center of Southington near the turnpikes and local hotels, was one of the only stores where residents could buy dry goods. The moment Bradley came to the center of Southington, he took an active role in building the community. In 1834, Amon Bradley, along with several other men in the community,

Young Merit Woodruff.

petitioned the Connecticut General Assembly for the incorporation of the Southington Fire Company.[11] In 1836, Amon and Sylvia took in a ward, a ten-year-old boy named Merrit Newell Woodruff, who would eventually become a crucial figure in the life of several members within the immediate Bradley family. Merrit came to Southington to attend local schools and boarded with Amon and Sylvia in their newly constructed home. Merrit's mother died when he was four. His father declared bankruptcy on his lumber business in New York in April 1842.[12] For eight years, Merrit lived with Amon and Sylvia, witnessing the birth of their first child, Franklin Barnes Bradley, on February 20, 1843 (Amon's birthday is February 20, 1812). Two years later, in 1844, Merrit left Southington in an attempt to revive his father's lumber business in New York, but the venture failed and shortly after he returned to Southington and began working for Amon once again as a clerk at his store. By the time Merrit rejoined him, Amon's real estate holdings in Southington included the Bradley House Hotel & Saloon, one of the most prominent restaurants and gathering in places in Southington for nearly a century. In 1849, Amon took Merrit as a partner at his store, and together they continued running the business until Amon retired in 1866, at which time Merrit took over the store himself. By that time, Merrit had purchased a home on High Street directly across the street from the Bradley Homestead, where he lived with his wife, Mary A. Smith; they had two children, Arthur and Edna.

THE RISE AND FALL OF THE BRADLEY BLOCK:
A CORNERSTONE OF SOUTHINGTON

Over the course of nineteen years from when Amon took up the role of postmaster in 1847 to about 1866, he held this powerful if not transformative position within a town teetering on the edge of the Second Industrial Revolution. The period between 1840 and 1860 in America was marked by significant economic, social and technological transformations, with road expansion playing a critical role in this era of change. As new roads were constructed out of necessity, existing ones were improved, such as the

This page, top: One of Southington's first fire trucks.

This page, bottom: Merit Woodruff's House on High Street would have been directly across from the museum today.

Opposite: Bradley House Hotel & Saloon. *From left to right*: Emma, Sylvia and Amon Bradley.

Farmington Canal Line and the Hartford and New Haven Turnpike, which gave locals easier access by coach to Hartford and New Haven. In fact, one of the main motivations for the Bradley House Hotel & Saloon was the fact that it was the perfect lodging stop along Route 10, formally known as the Cheshire Turnpike and still popular today.[13] Amon Bradley had acquired the Second Empire–style building on Main Street around 1840, making good on the interest of an unpaid loan he had given to the previous owner.

For many years, the Bradley House Hotel & Saloon was a fixture in the community and within the lives of the growing Bradley family members. Although the family did not run the establishment directly, they ensured that it offered the best meals and entertainment in Southington. Each October, Sylvia and Amon would celebrate their wedding anniversary at the Bradley House with a family and close friends, enjoying the lively atmosphere that had become synonymous with the establishment. The hotel gave the family a sense of pride and prominence in the community, as sixteen-year-old Alice Bradley noted in her diary on February 21, 1863: "Pa had his signs put up today; 'Bradley House' for the hotel and 'A. Bradley & Co.' for Lewis' store." Bradley House was often the center of social occasions. Amon's youngest daughter, Emma, noted on December 18, 1877, "We all attended the Y.M.S.C sociable in the Town Hall and had supper at the Bradley House. I went with Mr. Allis from N. Britain. Came home at 3:45.

Atkins and Severn's orchestra." During the holiday season in 1893, the Bradley House offered sleigh rides and hot and cold suppers and hosted a first-class dance hall, becoming the gathering place in the center of town. The establishment became so popular that in 1897 Amon announced his intention to expand it in the local paper.

The first of several expansions Amon would carry out led to the formation of the Bradley Block, which was completed by 1905. At ninety-three, Amon considered selling the property—who could blame him at that age? Ultimately, though, he did not sell the Bradley House or any of the buildings he owned on the land between Academy Street and Berlin Avenue. The entire block was owned by Amon Bradley and included the Bradley House Hotel & Saloon, a post office (which he eventually moved out of his home), a hall/store and a printing shop/photo studio/grocery that is now the Southington Community Cultural Arts Center. This block served as a central hub for the town's social, commercial and civic activities, making it a vital part of Southington's daily life in the nineteenth and early twentieth centuries.

It was also the alleged boardinghouse of the sixty-sixth governor of Connecticut, Marcus Holcomb, who came to Southington as a young attorney in the 1870s following the death of Southington's then probate judge, Amon's nephew Henry R. Bradley. Henry, a Yale graduate and lawyer, passed away at the age of thirty-eight in 1870 following complications from a lifelong illness. Alice Bradley, Amon's daughter, wrote about her first cousin's passing in her diary on July 22, 1870: "Charlie Bradley called this morning to tell us about cousin Henry; he is only just

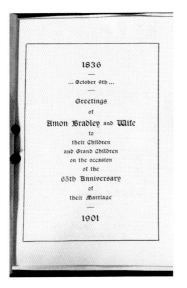

A menu from Amon and Sylvia's anniversary, held at the Bradley House.

Amon Bradley, circa 1860.

BRADLEY HOUSE,

H. BASSETT, Prop.

52 MAIN STREET, East Side of the Park, SOUTHINGTON, CONN.

First-Class Accommodations for the Traveling Public. Special Attention given to Table Boarders. Supper and Entertainments for Large or Small Parties at Short Notice. A full line of Ales, Liquors and Cigars.

LIVERY CONNECTED.   SPECIAL RATES TO DRUMMERS.

Undated advertisement for the Bradley House, a once popular attraction in Southington.

alive; Pa and Ma rode up this forenoon and staid till about 6 o'clock; he died at 3 ½ o'clock; did not have a very hard death; was not conscious."[14]

At the age of twenty-three, Alice was quick to observe many things in her diary, including when Holcomb arrived in town to replace her cousin on September 23, 1870: "The new lawyer [who opened the office Henry used to occupy] called to see Pa. He boards at the Hotel. Emma went with Nellie to a 'Temperance Lecture,' in the basement of the C. Church this eve." The significance of this visit being noted in Alice's diary suggests that Holcomb's need to gain Amon Bradley's approval, as Amon owned not only the hotel where Holcomb was boarding but also the probate office mentioned in Alice's entry. The office sat on Amon Bradley's property abutting the Unitarian Church, property he also owned, directly across from the Congregational Church on Pigweed Park (the soon-to-be beautified Town Green). This small office would once again become vacant in the 1890s and would become the playhouse of Amon's grandson Bradley Barnes.

Amon's ownership of nearly the entire block surrounding the Town Green reflected his gradual growth in influence on the town's development. However, by 1905, rumors had begun to circulate that Amon Bradley was contemplating the sale of his Main Street property. By 1919, the Bradley House had transformed and rebranded as the Southington Inn, navigating the challenges of Prohibition after a raid there in the early 1920s. The Bradley House continued to play a significant role in the town until its final days. After Amon Bradley's death in 1906, ownership of the house passed to his eldest son, Franklin. Sadly, Franklin died just a year later in 1907, before he could fully execute his father's will. As a result, all the assets,

Above: Bradley Barnes outside his playhouse on the Town Green.

Left: Thanksgiving dinner at the Bradley House, 1926.

including the Bradley House, were inherited by Franklin's wife, Julia Arnold Bradley. Julia later bequeathed the Bradley House to the Southington Hospital Corporation (read more about this in a later chapter). By 1930, the corporation was considering repurposing the Bradley House into an indoor golf course, but this endeavor left the building vacant for two years. The once-vibrant hotel stood silent and decaying as the tides of time shifted, and in 1931, the *Meriden Journal* announced the end of the Bradley House—the mighty eighty-five-year-old building was coming down. A little over a decade later, in 1941, the new Southington Town Hall was built on the same spot, marking the end of an era and the end of the Bradley Hotel & Saloon's memory in Southington.

BEYOND THE BRADLEY BLOCK: AMON BRADLEY'S INDUSTRIAL AND CIVIC LEGACY

As Southington continued to thrive into the late nineteenth century, the Bradley Block served as a bustling center of social and economic life. Amon Bradley's ambitions extended beyond his immediate surroundings (literally, as the Bradley Block was mere steps from his home). The expanding and improved roadways coupled with industrial developments provided fertile ground for those savvy in business like Amon to seize opportunities. No longer just a prominent local businessman, Amon began to play a pivotal role in Southington's broader industrial growth and political landscape. His influence would soon reach far beyond the Bradley House, as he took on new challenges in industry and public service, solidifying his legacy as one of Southington's most powerful and influential figures.

It is during this time that we see Amon transition from being a store owner, saloon owner and postmaster into a prominent industrialist and one of the most powerful men in Southington. In 1850, he became a Freemason with Southington's Friendship Lodge No. 33, F&AM. Freemasonry in America traces its roots back to the early eighteenth century, with the first Grand Lodge established in Pennsylvania in 1731. However, it wasn't until 1750 that Freemasonry found its footing in Connecticut, establishing lodges in New Haven and Hartford. The Grand Lodge of Connecticut was officially chartered in 1789, solidifying Freemasonry's presence in the state. In Southington, Freemasonry also thrived as early as 1795. Amon's involvement with Freemasonry through the Friendship Lodge No. 33,

F&AM, further expanded his influence in Southington and beyond. The Masons comprised Southington's most prominent residents. They often met at Amon's store and later in rooms at the Bradley House, intertwining their social activities with progressing personal business ventures. Through these connections, Amon found new opportunities to expand his influence in and beyond Southington. The relationships he built within the Masonic Lodge likely opened doors to larger enterprises, including his involvement with the Aetna Fire Insurance Company. As a board member, Amon played a key role in steering the company's growth, ensuring that it became a stable and reliable institution for policyholders like himself across the state. By 1850, when he became involved with the Aetna Fire Insurance Company, his real estate holdings had grown to include several establishments throughout town, including the expanding forthcoming Bradley Block (including Bradley House Hotel & Saloon and the attached post office). He also owned a portion of the block on the other side of Pigweed Park, as it was then known, or the Southington Town Green today.

During the nineteenth century, Hartford earned the nickname "Insurance Capital of the World" due to the early establishment of numerous insurance companies, including Aetna. Founded in 1819 by prominent Hartford businessmen concerned with the state's fire insurance industry, Aetna quickly grew to become a major player in the competitive market. The company's reputation was solidified after the Great New York City Fire of 1845, when Aetna, despite facing major financial losses, managed to pay all customer claims promptly, reinforcing its reputation throughout the young nation as a reliable and trustworthy insurer. Amon Bradley, with his business savvy and influence, was involved with Aetna Fire Insurance Company during a period when it expanded its services and cemented its role in Hartford's and the nation's insurance industry. Amon Bradley's involvement with Aetna was emblematic of his broader approach to business—strategic, forward-thinking and deeply connected to the economic pulse of the region. As a board member, Amon played a significant role in guiding Aetna through a period of rapid expansion and transformation.

Beyond his role at Aetna, Amon's investments extended into various sectors. His real estate ventures, particularly those connected to the Bradley Block and surrounding downtown area, positioned him as one of the most influential landowners in Southington. Between 1838 and 1869, Amon acquired, sold or mortgaged more than one hundred properties in Southington and nearly thirty in other towns and states. It was a normal activity for rent from those the family knew well to be dropped off at their home on North Main Street, with Amon's wife, Sylvia, noting in her February 24, 1879 diary entry: "Allie went to New Britain to spend a few days with Emma. Priest Dyer called to pay his rent. Pa went to a bank meeting in the eve."

And what did a renter of the Bradley family look like? Let's take a closer look at the Dyer family, whose time in Southington seems to have been limited to the 1880s. According to the 1880 census, Francis Dyer, a fifty-six-year-old clergyman originally from England, rented his home from Amon. Dyer had moved to Southington around 1877 with his wife, Elizabeth, and their two sons: William H., who in 1880 is listed as a twenty-year-old paper box maker, and Louis, a nineteen-year-old farm laborer. The Dyer family had relocated from New York to Connecticut, where Francis had served as a clergyman in Windham before settling in Southington. Although records suggest that he may have been affiliated with the Congregational Church, the specifics of Francis Dyer's church service in Southington remain unclear.[15] The Dyers' relationship with the Bradley family extended beyond a simple tenant-landlord dynamic. The regular visits from Francis Dyer to pay rent at the Bradley home, as noted in Sylvia Bradley's diary on several occasions, suggest a more personal connection between the families. These visits weren't just about paying rent—they were moments of connection that showed how business and community life were closely interwoven in small towns like Southington during the late nineteenth century. While the Dyers are frequently mentioned as delivering rent, it is likely that Amon personally visited many of his other tenants to collect their dues. However, the Dyers' relationship with the Bradley family appears to have been unique, possibly owing to Francis Dyer's role as a clergyman and his family's position within the community. The regularity of these visits and the personal nature of the interactions suggest that the Dyer family held a special place in the Bradleys' lives.

Amon's extensive real estate holdings, initially inherited through Sylvia's dowry when they married in 1834, were significantly expanded by him during the 1840s, '50s and '60s. This not only brought him considerable wealth but also gave him substantial influence over the development of Southington's infrastructure and economy. A typical mortgage deed from Amon included a clause stating that if a payment was not received on time, he would take possession of the property. These deeds often served as the bridge between his role as a former postmaster and his future role in securing the charter for the Southington Savings Bank in 1860. Amon frequently provided loans to local business owners and landholders, helping them secure their ventures. However, if the loan was not paid in full with the indicated interest by the agreed-on date, Amon would claim the property, thereby expanding his real estate empire. In some ways, Amon Bradley's business practices and his methodical way of accumulating real estate can be compared to the strategies used by Gilded Age robber barons like Jay Gould (1836–1892). Gould was notorious for his aggressive tactics in acquiring railroads, using financial leverage and strategic investments to expand his control over vast networks.[16] Similarly, Amon employed calculated mortgage agreements and loans to acquire property in Southington, steadily expanding his influence in the town. While Amon operated on a much smaller scale and within a more community-oriented context, both men exemplified the era's blend of ambition, financial cleverness and an unyielding drive to build personal empires. It was through these strategic loans and mortgage agreements that Amon was able to secure significant property throughout Southington. While he kept much of it, he did use these properties to encourage the expansion of available goods and services, including securing the town's water rights. His ability to manage and maintain relationships with tenants like the Dyers was a testament to his skill in balancing business with community engagement, ensuring that his ventures were not just profitable but also integral to the town's growth.

SOUTHINGTON CUTLERY COMPANY: BUILDING AN INDUSTRIAL LEGACY

In 1866, at the age of fifty-four, Amon Bradley announced his "retirement" from his shop, Amon Bradley & Company. But with the shop in the capable hands of his trusted former apprentice, Merrit Woodruff, this so-called retirement wasn't about slowing down. Instead, it marked a strategic shift in Amon's focus toward more profitable and expansive enterprises. Free from the day-to-day operations of the store, Amon redirected his energy toward Southington's growing industrial sector.

One of his most significant ventures during this period was his involvement in establishing the Southington Cutlery Company, which became a cornerstone of the town's industrial landscape. It was founded in 1867 by Amon and several other local investors, and initially stockholders and leaders met above Amon Bradley's store until the land they required abutting the New Haven and Northampton Railroad (often referred to as the "Canal Line") was secured by Amon later that same year. The location of the factory is less than half a mile from his home and remains there still today, known as Factory Square. Amon's efforts to establish the Southington

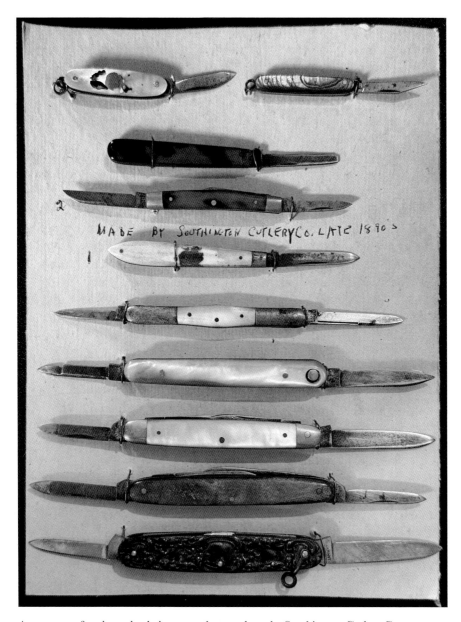

Assortment of early pocket knives or cutlery made at the Southington Cutlery Company.

Cutlery Company as a contender in the cutlery business in the state created jobs that attracted a diverse group of immigrants to downtown Southington. Pocket Cutlery, like many other industries, was established during the "free trade" period in America from approximately 1840 to 1889, a time when the U.S. economy was largely open to foreign competition with minimal tariffs and trade restrictions. This era allowed for the easy import and export of goods, fostering innovation and growth in industries like cutlery.

By the late nineteenth century, Connecticut had become a hub for cutlery manufacturing, with more than a dozen companies operating across the state. The industry's growth was fueled by Connecticut's diverse, skilled labor force, access to abundant waterpower from nearby rivers and well-developed rail lines like the New Haven and Northampton network, making the state a key player in the production of high-quality metal goods. Notable companies like the Empire Knife Company of Winsted and Meriden Britannia Company helped establish Connecticut's reputation in the cutlery industry before 1900.[17] From the start, Amon Bradley understood that producing high-quality products was key to the success of the Southington Cutlery Company. To ensure this, Amon constructed several multi-family homes near the factory and encouraged skilled English knife makers, many of whom had only just arrived in America, to come work for him. Initially, more than half of the employees were immigrants from England and Scotland, countries renowned for producing the finest cutlery in the world. By bringing in these craftsmen, Amon ensured that the Southington Cutlery Company could uphold the high standards set by the European manufacturers while also teaching local workers the intricate techniques of knife making, which had been an English specialty up until the end of the Civil War.

One such English immigrant, noted in the 1870 census, lived nearby and worked at the cutlery factory. At age twenty-seven, he moved to Southington with his wife, Margaret, also from England, who was twenty-six. They lived with their three children: Polly, age five, born in Pennsylvania; Charles, age three, born in Connecticut; and their youngest, Ellen, who was just six months old and born in May of that year. Living with them was a thirty-seven-year-old English-born renter, David Howe, who also worked in the cutlery shop. This glimpse into one household in 1870 shows how Amon not only brought in skilled workers to maintain the high quality and consistency of the Southington Cutlery Company's products but also welcomed their families. As these families settled in Southington, with women seeking work and children needing education, Amon's investment in his business naturally extended to investments in the community, driving the town's growth and development over time. As the Southington Cutlery Company continued to thrive, Amon's leadership guided the company through some major expansions. Founded with a capital stock of $50,000 in 1867, the company soon outgrew its original goals and began diversifying its product offerings.

The Southington Cutlery Company's first expansion in 1869 included the production of carriage bolts and wood screws, a move that reinforced the town's long-standing reputation as the nut and bolt manufacturing capital of America. Southington had been recognized for its expertise in bolt manufacturing since the 1830s, when the first patent for bolt manufacturing was issued here, solidifying its role as a leader in the manufacturing landscape. We often say that if Waterbury is the Brass City, Meriden the Silver City and Danbury the Hat City, then Southington is the Nut, Bolt and Screw Town. In 1883, however, the company decided to follow the market demands with the introduction of silver-plated holloware. These beautifully crafted pieces, often with intricate designs, catered to the desires of an emerging American middle class that could now purchase elegant and affordable tableware. This type of silver product was created by bonding a layer of silver over a base metal, typically pewter or nickel silver. The result was a durable and attractive product that mimicked the appearance of solid silver at a fraction of the cost.

The department might have done too good of a job producing these products, because it only operated for about ten years before it was sold in 1893 to the Meriden Britannia Company of Meriden, a national leader in the business of making beautiful silver plate. In 1898, the International Silver Company was formed, with its headquarters in Meriden, absorbing many of the small silver plating manufacturers scattered throughout Connecticut, including Meriden Britannia Company. Today, silver plate products might not fetch the same price as solid silver, but you'll likely spot them at your local thrift store; they still make for beautiful additions to any table. For well over a century, these pieces were the go-to gifts for weddings, anniversaries, birthdays and other cherished celebrations, bringing a touch of elegance to countless homes. So, while the resale value might not be sky-high, the charm and history behind each piece make them treasures worth keeping or gifting! Be sure to flip the item over to see if there is a stamp on the bottom indicating where it was made. Who knows, you may have a rare Southington Cutlery Company piece in your collection right now and not know it.

Amon's vision went far beyond just building a successful business. He was determined to turn Southington into an industrial hub. By 1883, when the

Left: Southington Cutlery Company silver plate teapot, circa 1890.

Right: Creamer made at the S. Cutlery Company, circa 1890.

company reorganized with a capital stock of $300,000, the factory buildings had expanded to cover a large area fronting Center Street and South Center Street. By this time, the workforce had shifted to include a significant number of Irish workers, a reflection of the broader immigration patterns of the late nineteenth century. Many Irish immigrants had fled famine and economic hardship in their homeland and found employment in American factories like the Southington Cutlery Company. By 1899, the production line had diversified to include razors, curry combs, tire bolts, stove bolts, wood screws and bicycle parts. Around this time, the factory began to see an influx of Southern Italian immigrants, who had initially arrived in Southington in small numbers during the 1870s. These immigrants were drawn to Southington by the promise of work and better living conditions, escaping poverty and political unrest in Italy. As the decades passed, their numbers grew significantly, and by the 1930s, nearly half of Southington's population was made up of Italian immigrants. This demographic shift mirrored broader trends in Connecticut, which has long been home to one of the largest Italian American communities in the country. In 1905, as these changes were taking root, the company ceased cutlery production altogether. By then, Amon had stepped back, having retired and sold nearly all his stock in the business several years earlier. This was likely due to a combination of internal politicking with the next generation of businessmen and his advancing age –by 1905, Amon Bradley was ninety-three years old. The company was renamed Southington Hardware Company in 1908 and continued to operate under this new name for many years, producing carpenter squares and tools.

Southington Hardware Company continued into the 1970s, when the company was sold to Elco Industries Inc. of Rockford, Illinois, in 1973. At the time, 170 people were employed by the company, which produced standard and special cold-headed fasteners. Similarly, Elco was a company that also produced fasteners and tools for the fasteners in the construction industry. Elco remained in the building until 1977. In the 1980s, the factory was updated as an early success story in revitalizing mill buildings in Connecticut. Today, it houses several prominent businesses, including a brewery, a vintage bar/arcade, a coffee shop, hair salons, dance studios, restaurants, a chocolate shop, a bakery and so much more.

SOUTHINGTON WATER COMPANY: A VITAL RESOURCE

As Southington's industries flourished and its population grew, the town's infrastructure needed to keep pace. Amon Bradley recognized that ensuring a reliable water supply was essential not only for his own investment's security but also for the safety and well-being of the town's residents. This understanding led him to play a crucial role in the creation and management of the Southington Water Company, a venture that not only had a lasting impact on the town's development but also continues today as the Southington Water Department. By 1880, Southington was a thriving industrial village with a population of 5,400, heavily reliant on its local water resources to support its growing industries and population. Major industries—including the Peck, Stow & Wilcox Company, Southington Cutlery Company and Aetna Nut Company—were dependent on water for their operations. With most of these factories—housed in large, wooden, multi-story buildings—fire protection became a significant concern, driving the push for a reliable water supply. Amon's own factory was susceptible to fire; his youngest child, Emma, noted in her diary on April 11, 1876, "The Cutlery shop took fire twice this eve."

The initial steps toward establishing a water company were taken by the Peck, Stow & Wilcox Company in 1881, leading to the formation of

THE SOUTHINGTON WATER CO.,

SUPPLY

Water for Domestic Uses,

FIRE AND MANUFACTURING PURPOSES.

Books for Collection and Application at the Office of the Company,

46 Center Street, Southington.

E. E. STOW, Pres't.   T. H. McKENZIE, Sec'y and Treas.

Undated advertisement promoting the Southington Water Company.

the Southington Water Works. The company was chartered by the state legislature in 1882, with an initial capital offering of $60,000. Despite some reluctance from residents to invest, the town voted to subscribe to $15,000 in stock, securing the funds needed to move forward with providing water service to a broader group of residents. The Southington Water Company's original waterworks building and well were strategically located across the street from Amon Bradley's home, adjacent to the Aetna Nut Company, a factory he helped establish later on. This location, near the heart of Southington's industrial center on Center Street, underscores Amon's deep involvement in overseeing the town's industry and essential infrastructure. As a director of the works, Amon played an instrumental role in the company's development, which included constructing a dam and installing pipelines to ensure that Southington's residents and businesses had access to clean water. While Amon played a significant role in establishing these various ventures, he often preferred to operate behind the scenes, avoiding public recognition and maintaining leadership roles for too long. Despite this, it was well known that he wielded considerable influence in the industries that helped shape Southington's development.

Chapter 3

THE VICTORIAN ERA
IN SOUTHINGTON

A house is not a home unless it contains food and fire
for the mind as well as the body.
—Benjamin Franklin

The Victorian era, spanning from the early nineteenth century to the turn of the twentieth century, was a time of grand ideas in art, literature and technology. The period comprised strict social codes, maximalist décor and, let's be honest, an overwhelming obsession with propriety. In Southington, these values took root in ways that were as unique as they were universal. This period wasn't just about crinolines, top hats and balls, although each occurred here in all its splendor. It was a time in which hard work, moral integrity and a bit of showmanship when it came to keeping up appearances could make or break your standing in the community.

For the Bradley family, the latter half of the Victorian era was a time of both challenge and opportunity. While Amon focused on expanding the family's influence and enterprises, the household ran like a well-oiled machine under the careful management of his wife, Sylvia Barnes Bradley. She ensured that everything from their three children's education to the pie crusts on her famous mince pies was done just right. Sylvia was the picture of Victorian womanhood, skillfully balancing the demands of a growing family, a bustling homestead and society's never-ending expectations. She did it all with a grace that turned heads every time she entered a room and a humor that made her a joy to be around. In this chapter, we pull back the heavy carpet curtains of the Barnes Museum to get a closer look at how Sylvia managed it all, offering a glimpse into the domestic life of a family that wasn't nearly poor but also wasn't so well off that they could sit around and do nothing all day.

SYLVIA BRADLEY'S DAILY LIFE
IN A VICTORIAN HOMESTEAD

Running a homestead in the mid-nineteenth century was not easy, especially for the matriarch of a bustling home. Each day was filled from dawn to dusk with a series of tasks that needed to be done—daunting to even the most organized of today's homemakers. Sylvia's mornings began with making the fire, which provided the necessary warmth for cooking and heating the home. From there, she would tackle a variety of household duties like laying or cleaning carpets, harvesting from the garden, canning and spending hours in the kitchen preparing food from scratch. The day didn't end there. Sylvia's evenings were often spent sewing, mending clothes or creating quilts. On top of it all, she raised three intelligent and kind children. Through the many diaries in our collection, we can piece together what an average day inside the Bradley home was like—sometimes even from multiple perspectives on the same day. The diaries offer rich details about daily life in the home and in the community, revealing that Sylvia was known for her signature mince pies and cider doughnuts and that she took laundry seriously as a means of keeping her family safe from illness. Each task she undertook was essential to the smooth running of the household—hard work and self-reliance that she later instilled in her children.

To truly understand the heartbeat of the Bradley household, we turn to one of the earliest diaries in our collection: the journal of Franklin Barnes Bradley, Amon and Sylvia's firstborn, who arrived in the world on February 20, 1843, on his father's birthday. At that time, Southington was a small but industrious town, with its economy centered on farming, tin manufacturing, cabinet and clock making and button production. As young Frank grew up on the Bradley Homestead on North Main Street, he documented his day in a diary, unwittingly recording a slice of mid-nineteenth-century American life. At ten years old, on November 3, 1853, he wrote, "I helped Mother put down carpets in the evening." This task wasn't just about laying carpets; it was a shared necessary task for winterizing the home and a glimpse into the

Left: Sylvia Barnes Bradley, circa 1863. *Right*: Franklin Bradley, circa 1863.

values Sylvia was attempting to instill in her children. Despite the family's relative means, with Amon's successful shop providing financial security, Sylvia believed in the importance of doing the work herself and in teaching her children to do the same.

In Victorian America, children were expected to contribute to the household, even those like Frank, who were fortunate enough to attend school, while others their age might be working in the local factories. Sylvia's approach reflected a broader cultural belief that children should be involved in the upkeep of the home, fostering a sense of responsibility and self-reliance. Frank didn't grow up waiting for someone else to do the work or sitting idle while his mother took care of everything. He was taught the value of rolling up his sleeves and getting things done, lessons that stuck with him throughout his life. Sylvia allowed her children to assist in all aspects of homesteading, including preparing food. She loved to cook, and through the collection we often find the children in the kitchen with her, as Frank will tell you on December 9, 1853, where he jotted down, "Mother and I stuffed sausages today." As he grew, Frank continued to lay carpet in the winter with his mother and help her in the kitchen when needed. He noted two years later at the age of twelve on November 10, 1855, "Mother cleaned the windows. I helped her put down two carpets." Carpets were

Antique Turkoman rug, circa 1870.

an essential element of Victorian domestic life, and we have many of them in the museum's collection. They served a practical purpose for many years, keeping the house warm and providing insulation, but as homes became more refined and ornate, carpets played a crucial role in adding warmth, comfort and a sense of luxury to the interiors. They provided insulation against the cold, especially in the harsh New England winters, and protected wooden floors from wear and tear. Carpets were also often seen as a symbol of status and taste, noted during afternoon visits for tea and often reflecting the wealth and social standing of the household. Maintenance was also a major undertaking, involving regular sweeping, beating and occasional cleaning—tasks that involved the entire family. From April 18, 1855, "I and Mother took up the carpet."

In 1849, when Frank was just six years old, his little sister, Alice, was born on October 22, just days before their mother Sylvia's thirty-first birthday on October 28. With Alice's arrival, Sylvia now had two children to care for on the homestead, and from a young age, Alice began documenting her day-to-day chores in her diary as well. Her earliest diary entry in the collection is from her eighth birthday in 1857: "Eighth anniversary of my birthday. I got up and made a fire." For a Victorian child, being able to make a fire was both a responsibility and a luxury, as it meant the family had a steady supply of chopped wood readily available. The following day, Alice noted that her father gifted her the journal as a birthday present, and from there, she was off, filling the pages with the lively observations of a young girl. Her entries are vivid and full of life and carry a tone that resonates with anyone who's ever been a tween, no matter the era. Her baby sister, Emma, had just been born on August 19 that same year, and she was so fond of her. On Saturday, October 24, eight-year-old Allie (as she was often referred to by friends and loved ones) wrote, "I built the fire and dressed myself. I took the baby for Mother, then she got up and dressed herself. Father did not get up very early this morning. I played my exercise on the piano. I ironed at night some of the baby's diapers." Anyone who has ever been a parent can probably imagine the scene that morning: a newborn in the house, an eager eight-year-old energetically practicing the piano and a fourteen-year-old Frank, who, in contrast, marked the occasion in his own diary with a simple, "Alice was eight years old today." You can almost hear Sylvia sighing in relief when Alice took the baby, if only for a few moments. This glimpse into Alice's world gives us a peek into the daily tasks she took on, even at such a young age. It shows how the expectations of the time shaped her daily life. Yet as the children grew up, their responsibilities shifted and varied. Fourteen-

Top: Thirteen-year-old Alice Bradley.

Bottom: Emma Bradley at the age of six.

year-old Franklin was training for his eventual path to take over his father's businesses and attend Yale. As he grew into young adulthood, his diary often noted the latest in town politics, such as on October 2, 1857, when he recorded, "The Democrats held a caucus in Father's hall, nominated Simeon Norton, Solomon Gridley, and Doctor Byington selectmen." Then there were major events like on November 5 of the same year, when "the store was broken open. The safe blown open with powder. Took a gold watch & father's diamond."

By the time the American Civil War broke out in 1861, Alice was eleven years old, and her diary captures the many changes occurring in her young life and that of her family's. Her entries from that year provide a window into the personal and public spheres that were beginning to intersect more deeply in the Bradley household due to Amon's influence beyond his store. For example, on March 6, 1861 she wrote, "Father went to Hartford to attend the congressional convention as a delegate." This entry hints at Amon's growing involvement in local and state politics, spurred by the looming conflict over enslavement in America. While Amon had always been a central figure in Southington's business community, the war brought new pressures and expectations, thrusting him into the state's political arena with greater intensity. During the Civil War, Amon Bradley was aligned with the Democratic Party, serving as a Democratic representative in the Connecticut legislature in 1861, 1863, 1864 and 1866. It's important to note that the Democratic Party at this time was not the party of Lincoln; in fact, it was deeply divided. Within the party, there were War Democrats who supported the Union's war efforts and Peace Democrats, often derogatorily called Copperheads, who opposed it. The Democratic Party in Connecticut was led by figures like Thomas H. Seymour (1807–1868), who served as thirty-sixth governor of Connecticut from 1850 to 1853 and was a vocal critic of the war. Seymour and his faction pushed for peace talks instead of a military win, believing that the war was harming the country. Months before the start of the war, on January 21, 1861, a young eleven-year-old Allie noted in her diary that her Aunt Diadamia, Amon Bradley's sister, had received a letter from her son Charles stating that the South was "burnt out." This likely referred to the economic strain the southern states were feeling as they faced the secession crisis. Alice's diary, filled with vivid descriptions of both everyday life and significant events, gives us a unique glimpse into how the war reshaped the Bradley family's world. She wrote of the war again two years later on April 4, 1863: "I made some sponge cake. Mr. Spofford & Mr. Stevens, two Democratic speakers, came to speak to the Democrats. They stayed overnight with us. Mr. Stevens gave me a copperhead pin."

A VICTORIAN KITCHEN:
THE HEART OF THE BRADLEY HOMESTEAD

As the turbulence of the Civil War loomed on the horizon, its impact began to ripple through the Bradley family and the town of Southington, subtly altering daily life. It was during these years, as the Bradley children grew into their adolescence and young adulthood, that the true demands of running a successful household during this period in history become evident. On January 12, 1863, thirteen-year-old Allie wrote in her diary, "Father was sick with pleurisy and did not go out of doors. In the evening, a peddler who carried silverware came in, and Father bought me a fruit knife and paid one dollar for it." Illness was a common and serious occurrence during this time, and it's no surprise that Allie made a note of it. However, what truly stands out is the glimpse it offers into Amon's character; even while sick, Amon couldn't resist supporting a fellow peddler, despite having left the peddling business three decades earlier. Meanwhile, their eldest child, Franklin Bradley, was away at Yale, preparing for his upcoming graduation in the spring of 1863. Throughout the 1860s, Allie's diaries paint a picture of a life that, on the surface, seems not too different from that of any typical thirteen-year-old. Her days were filled with attending school, practicing music, collecting money for a new bell at Lewis Academy and helping her mother around the house. Yet her entries often offer a deeper glimpse into her world, particularly when she mentions the daily tasks she or Sylvia accomplished. For instance, on April 1, 1864, she wrote, "The Republicans had a caucus this evening and nominated William Willcox as first Representative and Enos Stow as second. Dr. Hart as Judge of Probate. Mother made some splendid soft soap today." Allie gave us the

Lewis Academy, located just steps from the Bradley Homestead.

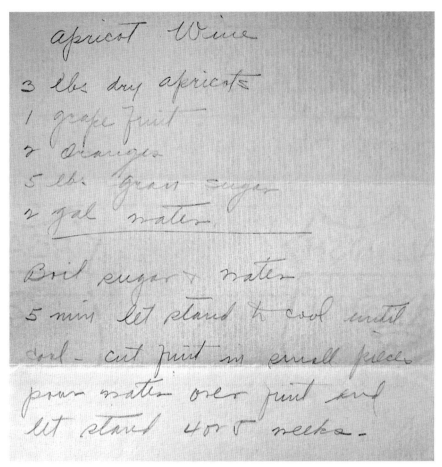

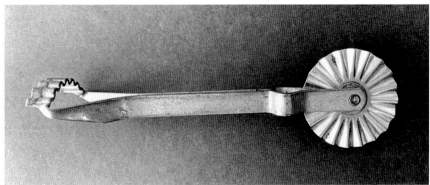

Top: Sylvia Bradley's apricot wine recipe.

Bottom: Specialty tool for pie making, circa 1860.

essential happenings in Southington that day but finished with what clearly stood out the most to her: her mother's skill in homesteading.

Making soap in 1864 was no small task. It was a hands-on, time-consuming process that began with rendering fat from animals like cows or pigs into tallow. This tallow was then mixed with lye, which was made by soaking the ashes from burnt wood in water. The mixture had to be carefully cooked and stirred until it thickened into soap, which was then poured into molds to set. Sylvia would have learned how to do this at a young age on her father Truman Barnes's farm. Even at forty-six years old (beyond the age of the average life expectancy for women), she was still taking on these labor-intensive tasks, including making their own candles, preserving jams, canning pickles, brewing beer and making wine. Much of this work took place in the summer kitchen—its own small outbuilding designed to keep the heat and odors of these chores from overwhelming the main house. This single-room building, built alongside the house in 1836, is equipped with a colonial hearth and fireplace and became Sylvia's go-to spot for all her chores—from a huge urn to do laundry and make soap to a canning table and closet for storage and a large tub for doing laundry. These tasks were essential for keeping the family clean, healthy and fed. Sylvia didn't just prepare meals here; she taught her children life skills, from cooking to maintaining the household. Allie noted it on October 29, 1870: "We arranged the plants in the dining room, moved the cook stove into the sink-room and the morning-glory into the kitchen today. Ma received a letter from Mrs. Wilcox, also a box by express containing a very handsome butter dish as a present." Her sister, Emma, wrote on the same day but offered a brief bit of context: "Truman Judd came and helped us put up the morning-glory stove." A morning glory, also known as a base-burning stove, was a staple type of coal-burning stove in nearly every home in the late nineteenth century, designed to maintain a steady heat over long periods. During warmer months, stoves like these were often moved from the main house to the summer kitchen to keep the main house cool. Today, it remains the one room at the Barnes Museum has least changed since the 1840s. In the 1870s, Sylvia used the fireplace and small stove in the summer kitchen for many different home-related tasks like boiling water for laundry, canning fruits and vegetables and baking her specialty: pies. But the kitchen was more than just a functional space for Sylvia; like it is for many of us still today, the kitchen can be the heart of a home, where the children sat by their mother's feet as she completed daily tasks to much later as women sewing, canning and preserving with her side by side. The summer kitchen, with its thoughtful design, eventually became attached to the main house as Amon added rooms and expanded his family home over the years.

A NEW ERA BEGINS:
THE BRADLEY-BARNES MARRIAGES

As the 1870s unfolded, the Bradley household experienced significant changes, particularly with the marriages of the Bradley children. The first of Amon and Sylvia's children to marry came on June 16, 1869, when Franklin married Julia Arnold of New Britain. Frank's younger sister Allie, just sixteen, provided a lengthy description of the events that day: "Just after dinner Father, Mother Emma and I went over to the Humphrey House in New Britain to wait for a hack to take us to the church to see Frank & Julia and Cornelia & Mr. Walker married. Mr. Walker's Father [the Baptist pastor] performed the ceremony; Mr. Goodell [the regular pastor of the South Church] stood by. They were not married in the Baptist Church as it is being re-built….A number of Southington people were present. After the ceremony, Ma, Pa Emma and I rode up to Mr. Fred Stanley's to see the presents; we staid a few minutes, and then started for home. The bridal party went to Berlin to take the cars, directly after the ceremony was performed." Almost exactly nine months later, their son, Amon Edward Bradley, was born on April 5, 1870, in Cleveland, Ohio, where his father was running the Cleveland Eyelet Company. Sylvia had gone out there to ensure the safe arrival of her first grandchild, while Allie waited patiently at their North Main Street home back in Southington. The following day, on April 6, 1870, Allie wrote, "Received a letter from Ma saying Julia had a fine boy; born last Tuesday morning about 5 o'clock. I am an aunt; Ahem!"

The second of the Bradley children to marry was Allie herself in 1873, when she wed her third cousin Norman Barnes, marking a new chapter not just for her but for the entire Bradley Homestead. Their love story is one for the ages, more reminiscent of *Romeo and Juliet* than that of a love novel from the Victorian era. Norman is first mentioned by Allie in her 1861 diaries when he stops in for a visit with the family. Norman A. Barnes was born on August 16, 1843, to Joel and Anna Clark Barnes in the Marion village within Southington. Having been born in town the same

Left: Julia Arnold Bradley, circa 1876. *Right*: Norman Barnes.

year as Franklin Bradley, Norman attended local schools with Frank and later Lewis Academy. It was at Lewis Academy where he began teaching at the age of nineteen, a position he held there for about eight years. What began as a friendship between student and tutor with Allie grew into a deep romantic connection. Despite the strong initial opposition from some members in Alice's family, the two could not be separated and continued to write to each other while Norman attempted a clerkship position in New York. He hoped by leaving his position as a teacher he could prove himself able in a more profitable career. While it's unclear exactly when their relationship shifted from friendship to romance, letters exchanged between them in October 1863, when Alice was just thirteen, hint at the blossoming of romantic feelings. In a letter from New York dated October 12, 1863, Norman wrote to Alice, "Here I am all alone and I must confess that I am a little homesick. How I would like at this moment to step into your place and see you, but cannot." Just two weeks later, on October 26, Alice replied from Southington with equal affection: "Thanksgiving is coming and I am really glad, for I suppose you are coming home then.

It seems as though I had not seen you in a long, long time. We miss you very much, particularly myself as I have no one like you to play with at the table." Her diary entries from that year further reflect the depth of her teenage infatuation with Norman. On January 24, she noted, "I went up to visit Norman's school in the forenoon;" A few weeks later, on February 14, she noted fondly, "I had a nice time down to Norman's. He made me a black ring. We made popcorn balls." Norman's connection with the Bradley family deepened over time, as evidenced by Alice's April 29 entry: "Father, Mother, sister, brother, myself and Norman Barnes went to the ball. I danced for the first time at a ball. I danced with Brother once and with James Parker twice." Notice how she did not dance with her future husband. In April of that same year, Norman began working as a clerk at Amon Bradley & Company, boarding with the family for several months. From then on, he became a regular presence in the Bradley Homestead and a near daily presence in Allie's diaries.

In 1868, after years of a growing bond, Norman wrote a heartfelt letter to Amon and Sylvia Bradley, seeking their permission to marry their daughter. The letter came as no surprise, for the family knew about their mutual infatuation for some time. In this letter, he expressed his love for her and his desire to be part of the family, understanding the need to provide her with the life she was accustomed to. Here follows an excerpt from the letter:

> But this I am bound to do until forbidden by Father or Mother. Allie and myself have talked of these things often. She is fully convinced that I love her with my whole heart, I am convinced that she loves me with her whole heart. Whence we ask in all earnestness that we may consider ourselves as engaged to each other, as Man and Wife, or until we are joined in the holy bonds of Matrimony, when we then would feel the full force and realize the meaning of the words Companions for Life. Pray give this earnest and careful consideration; make it the subject of much thought before you answer. But we truly feel as if it should be of necessity be answered. For certainly it would be decidedly wrong for me to win more of her affection or she of mine, and then be separated forever; it would perchance ruin us both for the remainder of Life. But this we hope will not be. We trust our petition will be granted; and still we would not wish it granted if it should be the means of making a life-long distrust on the Family, or the cause of biter enmity for the remainder of Life's journey. Although it would be hard, better hard to give each other up.

Leaving him with little option, Amon, being ever the pragmatic businessman, took Norman even further under his wing, ensuring that Norman was well equipped to support his eldest daughter before granting his blessing. By 1870, Norman's teaching career was far behind him, as he had become firmly established in Southington's business world, holding positions such as the registrar of voters for town elections and secretary of the Atwater Manufacturing Company. Their wedding took place on October 9, 1873, at the First Congregational Church in Southington, a date chosen out of fondness, as it was the same date as the anniversary of Amon and Sylvia's marriage. Alice's diary entry from that day reflects her joy and the significance of the occasion: "Today is my wedding day, and pleasant it is, and I am so thankful too. I have a great many flowers given by my friends and neighbors, and a nice lot of bridal gifts, many more than I mentioned, in this book." Following their wedding, Alice and Norman honeymooned in New York, enjoying the sights and culture of the city, including a performance at Booth's Theatre. Their honeymoon was a brief escape before returning to Southington, where they would live with Alice's parents for the next decade in what Allie referred to in her diary as the North Wing of the house. It was a common practice in Victorian America for the children to remain with their parents after marriage until a home could be secured for themselves. As they settled into married life, Alice and Norman brought their own touches to the Bradley Homestead, blending their tastes with the established traditions of the house. They were both active in social circles, with Alice being a founder of the Clotho Society, which began as a community fundraising group and later became something like a drama club. Norman, too, was involved in social and political activities, and their shared love of performance and community involvement became a hallmark of their life together. In 1882, just before the birth of their son, Bradley Barnes, they moved into a new home on the Southington Town Green on property owned by Amon.

Alice Bradley in her wedding dress. When she died, she was buried in it, which is why we do not have it today.

Above: Norman Barnes's house on the Town Green on property formerly owned by Amon.

Left, from left to right: Julia, Franklin, Sylvia and Amon, with Edward and Emma standing on the porch of the homestead.

Emma Bradley, the youngest daughter of Amon and Sylvia, was naturally the last to marry, on October 19, 1888, at the age of thirty-three. She married Edward Yeomans of Litchfield, Connecticut, who was known for operating the Southington Medicine Company on Railroad Avenue for many years. Affectionately called "Yeomie" by the family, Edward was known as a dandy, someone who took great pride in his appearance, which is evident from his well-dressed portrait. Beyond their mutual flair for fashion, he and Emma were also great lovers of animals, and Yeomie earned a reputation in Southington as a horseman. Later in life, he owned and operated the local livery and hack stable behind the Bradley House Hotel & Saloon, situated where the Gura Building stands today, on the corner of Berlin Avenue and Main Street. Emma and Edward Yeomans enjoyed seventeen happy years of marriage. Ten of these years were unfortunately spent struggling with Yeomie's epilepsy. Emma and Edward sought various treatments across New England from the mountains to the sea, attempting to manage his condition as best as they could. When his health allowed, he continued to ride through town with his favorite horse, visiting friends and family, maintaining as much normalcy as possible. Living with epilepsy during the Victorian era was extremely difficult. During the decade leading up to his death in 1905, he rarely left the house, as he struggled with frequent seizures. Emma and Yeomie lived with Amon and Sylvia in the family home on North Main Street.

Although Emma later remarried to Henry Newell in 1906, she never forgot her first husband. In her will, Emma made numerous charitable donations that reached every corner of the Southington community. She bequeathed more than $30,000 to three cemeteries in town and $1,000 to each church in Southington. Notably, she left $5,000 to the First Congregational Church to install a chime of bells in its belfry as a memorial, inscribed as a "Gift from Emma Bradley Yeomans Newell." Emma's generosity extended to other public works still relevant today. She left $5,000 to the Town of Southington for the erection of a historical building known as the Sylvia Bradley Memorial, which was added as a wing to the public library and now houses the Southington Historical Society. Additionally, she allocated $5,000 for a drinking fountain for horses in the center of Southington and another in Plantsville, both in memory of her first husband, Edward S. Yeomans, inscribed "A Lover of Animals."

Henry Newell, Emma's second husband, was born in Southington as Henry Blood on April 7, 1851. After his parents separated, he took his mother's maiden name. Henry worked as a traveling salesman for several of

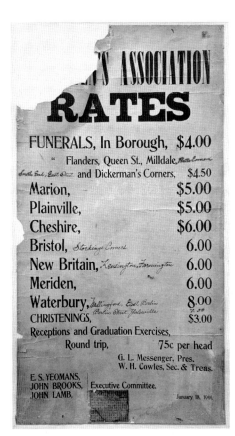

Left: Renting rates for horses and carriages from the Liveryman's Association.

Below: Emma Bradley and Henry Newell's home on Main Street is the site where the Elks organization gathers today.

Southington's bolt manufacturers. His mother, Martha Newell, was born in Southington in 1820, and Henry lived with her in the village of Plantsville, taking care of her during her declining health until her death in 1903. By the time Henry married Emma in 1906, they had known each other for years through their mutual involvement in the town. Their home on Main Street, not far from the Bradley Homestead, was one of the largest on the block, with a garden renowned throughout the state. That home, now known as the Elks Lodge, still retains much of its character despite some modifications.

Emma passed away at the age of sixty-three on November 21, 1917, at 4:00 a.m., and Henry died the following day at 1:00 p.m., reportedly from the shock of losing his wife. In his will, he left everything to Emma, and in hers, most of her estate was left to him. At the time of her death, Emma was noted as "the richest woman in Southington." True to her generous nature, she ensured that her wealth was distributed among friends, family and the broader Southington community. Her legacy is still felt today, as nearly every corner of Southington benefited from her philanthropy.

As the Victorian era ended, the Bradley family exemplified the period, defined by values of hard work, both in business and at home. While the Bradley women didn't hold traditional jobs, they were the backbone of the household, managing social affairs and keeping the house running—a role that many successful men of that time relied on their wives and children to fulfill. The Bradleys were respected in Southington because they gave respect. They earned it by giving it, whether in business dealings or social interactions, and this is the foundation that allowed Frank, Alice and Emma to carry forward the family legacy.

CHAPTER 4

FROM HEIR TO HEIRLOOM

Barnes Inheritance

As the Victorian era came to a close and the new century beckoned, the Bradley family found itself in the position to loosen the reins Amon spent so long mastering. The marriages of Frank, Alice and Emma were testaments to Sylvia and Amon's efforts to raise children who were not only capable but also generous. Now, with a new generation emerging, Amon Edward Bradley and a young Bradley Barnes were getting ready to leave their own marks on Southington. From an early age, both men were active members of the community. Young Bradley Barnes could often be found in his playhouse on the Town Green, which occupied his late uncle's former probate court office—a space once held by Marcus Holcomb, who would go on to become Connecticut's sixty-sixth governor. Bradley's playhouse symbolized the family's wealth and real estate hold on the town's center, but it was also a reflection of the deep love and support Bradley received from his family, as we can read in one of his earliest diary entries.

On January 27, 1892, he wrote, "I am nine years old today. Papa and Mama put $50 in the bank as they do every birthday. I had a writing pad, a little Jr. Rochester lamp, a box of paints, a cover for my little milking stool, a Book of silver pen-holder and pencil, a gold toothpick, perfume, candy, handkerchief, necktie, etc. Mama had Anna and Walter here to tea; they brought me a lovely birthday cake, and Mama had the baker make one for me with B.H.B. 1883–1892 on it. Nellie Curtiss brought me a little book, so we asked her to stay to tea. Grandma sent me a bouquet and some Florida oranges."

In today's terms, the $50 deposit Bradley received would be equivalent to about $1,600, which is a pretty big sum for a nine-year-old boy. Bradley loved his parents deeply and felt a strong connection with his grandparents. His diary entries from May 1895 at the age of twelve capture the simple joys of their everyday life. On May 8, Bradley noted, "After tea, I went up for Grandma, who is going with Papa, Mama, and I to hear the Little Vernon Brothers in the Town Hall." For many years, all the local entertainment was either in someone's private hall, two of which Amon Bradley owned, or at the Congregational Church or town hall. Just a few days later, on May 12, Bradley proudly jotted, "I got the one-hundredth egg from my chickens today." Some of these entries, though brief, paint us a picture of a boy deeply rooted in his family's traditions and daily life, foreshadowing how important preserving his family's legacy would be to him in later years. For many years, they lived happily like this, close in proximity and in their hearts until life took a tragic turn in June 1897 with the sudden death of forty-seven-year-old Alice Bradley Barnes, shaking the family to the core. For many years, it was a humble brag each time Amon and Sylvia celebrated their anniversary that the "chain of life" in their family had remained unbroken. For the time, death was a common daily occurrence, with the names of friends, loved ones and notable residents of the community recorded daily in the family member's diaries. Losing Allie was devastating. Although she had been battling an illness for some time, her death still came as a shock, leaving a void that would never truly be filled again. The exact cause of her illness remains unclear in the museum's archives, although there are hints that it might have stemmed from an injury she sustained during an accident on a swing when she was younger. This tragic event is barely acknowledged in fourteen-year-old Bradley's 1897 diary, a big difference from his more detailed entries from previous years. That year, his writing became much more brief, focusing on moments with his grandparents, sledding with his father and then abruptly ending in May, just one month before Alice's passing.

Alice loved her only child deeply, and they shared a close bond.

This shift in tone and the eventual end of Bradley's diary entries in 1897 suggest the deep emotional impact of his mother's illness and subsequent death. Bradley and his mother were close beyond the words I could describe to you here. Despite the wealth of artifacts and memories Bradley would later meticulously preserve, Alice's death at such a pivotal time in his young life seems to have been quietly tucked away in the broader narrative of the Barnes family. Mental health wasn't a subject much broached. Norman, Bradley's father, became somewhat overprotective of Bradley after Alice's passing, often noting in his letters to him his anxieties around Bradley getting unexpectedly ill or finding himself in dangerous situations. This didn't stop Bradley from growing into a curious young man eager to explore all that the new century had to offer.

After Alice's passing, the concept of inheritance likely took on profound significance for the Bradley and Barnes families. For them, inheritance was much more than wealth; it was a means of safeguarding the family's history, values and place in Southington. This emphasis on legacy became even more pressing after the loss of Sylvia in 1903. A day or two after Thanksgiving that year, Sylvia became ill with a hard cold, and the doctor feared that pneumonia would develop. As she had suffered from heart trouble for a few years, panic swept through the family. Despite a brief moment of cheerfulness on the morning of her death, Sylvia passed away on December 11, 1903, at the age of eighty-five. At the time, her son Franklin Barnes Bradley lived nearby, and Emma, Mrs. Edward Yeomans, resided at the Bradley Homestead with her husband. With the loss of both Alice and Sylvia, capital, politics and industrialism fell secondary to the responsibility Amon Bradley felt to preserve the family's legacy. Ever the astute businessman, Amon understood that the preservation of his family's legacy required meticulous planning. His foresight and strategic thinking were evident in the provisions he made in his will, a document he once claimed he would never have, ensuring that the wealth he accumulated over his lifetime would be distributed in a way that not only provided for his family but also preserved all that he had worked so hard to establish in Southington.

AMON'S WILL AND ESTATE

Following the death of his wife, Sylvia, in 1903, Amon Bradley meticulously planned the distribution of his estate to ensure that his family's legacy in Southington would be preserved and strengthened. He passed away on

August 13, 1906, at the age of ninety-seven. Newspapers were quick to speculate on what would happen to his money. For several weeks, publications from Hartford to Bridgeport across the state of Connecticut speculated on what would happen to the estate of "Southington's Richest Man." Rumors circulated that he didn't have a will and then that he did have one. Like something out of a Dickens novel, some members of the community went so far as to say that they were glad, for it meant they had more time to accumulate the money to pay the debts they owed to him, knowing that they would now likely be working with a different member of the Bradley family. Ultimately, Amon's estate was valued at more than $613,000, which in

James H. Pratt, executor of Amon's will and trusted family friend.

1906 would be equivalent to about $20 million today, considering inflation. This was a massive sum for a farmer turned peddler turned capitalist and industrialist, but not quite on par with the fortunes amassed during the Gilded Age by the elite of, say, Newport, Rhode Island.

A significant portion of Amon's wealth was held in real estate, stocks and bonds. The bulk of his estate included $420,352 in stocks and bonds, many of which were kept and distributed to family, ensuring that they would continue to benefit from the investments he made throughout his life. Amon also held substantial amounts in savings, mortgages and promissory notes, which further diversified the family's financial portfolio. His real estate holdings were mostly in Southington and were carefully distributed among his family members, each allocation reflecting both a practical and symbolic connection to the family's history in Southington. The W.S. Gould store building and the old Unitarian Church property, key landmarks on the Town Green for many years, although they no longer remain today, were part of Amon's extensive portfolio and bequeathed to Norman and Bradley Barnes. Norman's house was on the same block. The Bradley Block, which included the House Hotel and the livery property on the corner of Berlin Avenue and Main Street, once operated by Edward Yeomans, was passed down to Amon's eldest son, Franklin Bradley.

By the time of his father's passing, Franklin was sixty-three years old and facing his own health challenges. Although he inherited his father's properties, Franklin had long since moved away from the manufacturing side of the

Soldiers and Sailors Monument on the Southington Town Green.

family business. In the 1860s, Franklin helped establish the Cleveland Eyelet Company in Ohio and later became connected to the Southington Cutlery Company with the formation of the Southington Eyelet Company. By the early 1900s, these two businesses had merged to become the Southington Hardware Company. At that time, Franklin stepped back from manufacturing to pursue a career in finance, running a brokerage firm out of a prominent building in Hartford. Naturally, Amon had initially named Franklin as the executor of his will, with Franklin's firm, the Hartford Securities Company, assisting in the estate's distribution. However, after Frank's death in March 1907, a new executor of Amon's estate was needed. While Hartford Securities was already involved in managing the estate and was eager to complete the process, most of the living parties interested in the estate—namely, Bradley, Julia and Emma—were uncomfortable with the firm continuing and wanted

Bradley Chapel at Oak Hill remains today and is a frequent stop on our fall walking tours.

someone closer to home to oversee matters. They appointed Southington native James H. Pratt (1853–1937), a lifelong resident and a well-regarded industrialist, who served as president of Atwater Manufacturing Company, Aetna Nut Company and Southington Hardware Company—all businesses that had strong ties to Amon Bradley.

One of the most significant properties in Amon's estate was the Bradley House on the Town Green, which ultimately came under the care of Franklin's widow, Julia Arnold Bradley. This house, along with other properties, including parcels on Main Street, Bristol Street and Meriden Avenue, were distributed among various family members. Beyond real estate, Amon ensured the financial well-being of his children and grandchildren. His eldest grandson, Frank and Julia's son, Amon Edward Bradley, was entrusted with $20,000, held in trust. By the time of his father Franklin's death in 1907, Amon Edward was thirty-six years old and married and had followed in his father's footsteps by working alongside him in the brokerage business. The remainder of Amon's estate was divided among his youngest daughter, Emma Bradley Yeomans, and his only other grandson, Bradley H. Barnes. Bradley's share was to be given in parts over time, more of Amon's careful planning. Amon's will was more than just a division of his long-accumulated assets—it was a blueprint for the family's future, designed to protect the wealth and influence he had amassed while ensuring that the Bradley name remained prominent in the Southington social and business community.

Bradley Homestead, home to Bradley and Leila circa 1920.

After Amon's passing, the Bradley Homestead, which would later become the Barnes Museum, was entirely given to Emma in the settlement of the estate. Plans for the Bradley, Yeomans, Barnes Memorial Chapel inside Oak Hill Cemetery were set in motion shortly after Franklin Bradley's unexpected death in 1907, with Emma Bradley Yeomans, Bradley Barnes, Julia Arnold and Merrit Woodruff leading the charge. This chapel, along with a receiving vault, was intended to honor the memory of the Bradley family and their close relations. Construction was completed in May 1908, and the chapel served a dual purpose: it was both a tribute to the family's legacy and a place where the community could come to honor their own loved ones, a function it still provides today.

Later that same year, in October 1907, Emma sold her interest in the Bradley Homestead to her twenty-four-year-old nephew, Bradley H. Barnes. Following his graduation from nearby Meriden Pequod Business College in 1901, Bradley found himself increasingly taking on more significant roles within the family's business ventures, including becoming vice-president of the Atwater Manufacturing Company. When Bradley assumed stewardship of the homestead, he knew the purpose that it would serve: a home for him and his soon-to-be wife, Leila Upson, marking a critical turning point in this story.

THE RENOVATION OF THE BRADLEY HOMESTEAD

In October 1907, Emma Bradley Yeomans made the decision to sell her inheritance in the Bradley Homestead to her then twenty-four-year-old nephew, Bradley H. Barnes. Bradley was then a young man who enjoyed cars, horses, sailboats and moving pictures; in his spare time, he served as vice-president of the Atwater Manufacturing Company. With the homestead now under his care, Bradley was eager for it to become a stately home for him and his childhood friend and soon-to-be wife, Leila Upson. Taking over the homestead meant more to Bradley than just inheriting his grandparents' house—it was about preserving the legacy of one of Southington's most respected families. Working with his father Norman's guidance, Bradley began planning for his future at 85 North Main Street, focusing on how he could modernize the homestead while maintaining its historic integrity and character. Leila, who was deeply rooted in Southington herself and grew up just down the street from the Bradley Homestead, shared in Bradley's vison for the house and his commitment to his family's legacy. Together, they embarked on a journey to transform the Bradley Homestead into their marital home, promising to marry once the house was complete and they could move in.

By the time Bradley inherited the homestead, the property had undergone significant transformations, far removed from the modest 1836 structure with which we began this story. The expansion in the mid-1870s, which included the addition of the "North Wing," made space for Alice and Norman after their marriage. This extension, which continued modestly into the 1880s, introduced three bedrooms on the second floor, a downstairs living room, a dining room and, from what we can gather (although any physical trace of it has disappeared since the 1940s), a billiard room off the dining room that connected the main house to the summer kitchen. We often tell guests that the house feels larger on the inside than it appears from the outside thanks to the seventeen rooms you can explore today. From an exterior view, it sometimes seems like there are two separate houses connected: the original 1836 Greek Revival structure envisioned by Amon and the 1870s addition extending westward. You wouldn't know it today, as these sections blend seamlessly, creating one beautifully grand home.

While earlier renovations carried out by Amon came from necessity due to the growth of the family, the new renovations by Bradley were necessary to modernize the home with all the luxuries of the twentieth century. To bring Bradley's vision to life, he sought the expertise of J. Edgar Norris, a well-regarded architect from Worcester, Massachusetts. Correspondence between Bradley and Norris throughout 1909 reveal their shared commitment to transforming the Bradley Homestead into a residence that reflected both wealth and refined taste, as he aimed to create a house that would stand out as a landmark in Southington. Norris could hardly know when making that statement in 1909 that he was speaking about a future museum! Norris assured Bradley in their exchanges that the renovation would result in a home that was both elegant and comfortable, fitting for a man of Bradley's status. "It will make a very aristocratic and homelike looking house, like the residence of a wealthy man such as it will be," Norris explained. In turn, Bradley's commitment to the project was evident in his timely responses and willingness to collaborate closely with Norris. For instance, on August 13, 1909, Bradley enclosed a $100 payment and

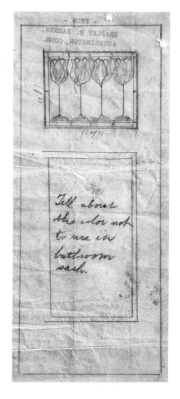

requested a receipt, demonstrating his active involvement in the renovation process. Norris outlined detailed plans that included modern amenities, while ensuring the house retained its dignified character. He mentioned the integration of plumbing, electric wiring and leaded glass—cutting-edge design features at the time that remain intact today. His focus was on achieving a balance between luxury and comfort, something to show off to guests but also enjoy. The aim of the renovations was to make the home more livable but also more impressive.

Norris managed every detail of the renovation, from drafting blueprints to selecting materials and coordinating with local contractors. He made sure to include the names Bradley's father, Norman, had recommended, and naturally both Norman and Bradley were mindful of the costs involved, corresponding about different materials throughout. Norris assured him that the renovation would stay within budget but also elevate the home. By the summer of 1909, the plans were in full swing. Bradley's letters to Norris reveal a very collaborative relationship, with both men fully invested in the project, and while Bradley traveled and attended conference on nut and bolt

Opposite: Etching of lead glass from Norris to Bradley, with notes. Can be seen throughout the museum today.

Left: Photo of maybe the fireplace in the Receiving Room or of the interior today.

Below: Leila in the conservatory, taken by Brad in 1911.

manufacturing, Norris made regular trips to Southington to oversee progress and make necessary adjustments.

The interior renovations were completed by the summer of 1910, just in time for Bradley's marriage to Leila on October 6, 1910, a date likely chosen to honor the other October anniversaries in the family. The newly transformed homestead now featured three internal bathrooms, a second-floor dressing room designed specifically for Leila, an upstairs office, new leaded glass on the front door and a large bay window in the living room. Leila took an active role in selecting the home's décor, from the wallpaper in each room to the custom plaster and wood moldings that adorn the fireplaces. The most significant addition for Leila was the conservatory, a space where she could nurture her cherished plants. This new room, filled with natural light, quickly became her sanctuary. In early April 1911, just as the first daffodils began to bloom in the garden, Bradley captured a photograph of Leila standing in the doorway of the conservatory. The image, taken with a clear sense of pride and love, shows Leila in a moment of peace, surrounded by the beauty she had helped create. Each element of this renovation, including the conservatory, remains intact today and continues to be a highlight during tours of the museum.

WIFE AND ARTIST: LEILA UPSON BARNES

Leila Upson Barnes, born on October 31, 1884, in Southington, was the eldest child of Frank Root Upson and Hattie Holcomb Upson. Her father, Frank, co-owned the Upson Brothers Grocery, one of the first grocers in Southington. The store was located on Center Street, where the future Oxley Drug Store would be, and was a hub of community activity. Frank and his brother William greeted customers, knew their weekly orders and offered a more specialized shopping experience than the general stores of the past. Unlike the general stores of the past like Amon Bradley's, which offered a mix of things from hardware to textiles, Upson Brothers Grocery focused specifically on food and household necessities like cleaning supplies. The store was known for its impressive displays of canned goods, a relatively new convenience at the time. These canned goods were often arranged in eye-catching pyramids, showcasing how modern marvels had transformed shopping. Customers would come in and greet Frank's familiar face, hand over their list and come back or wait while the grocer gathered and packaged everything, eliminating today's problem of browsing aisles for that one missing ingredient. In the 1890s, retail stores, like the Upson Brothers, often used daring window displays with shocking attractions such as the display of a tarantula in the shop window in 1894! Aside from offering groceries, the store also boasted a selection of toiletries, including perfumes. By 1896, the store had embraced modernity by introducing phone orders for customer convenience, as advertised in the local paper the *Southington Phoenix*. As a child, Leila developed a deep appreciation for art and nature, passions that would define her life. One of the earliest etchings in the museum's collection is of the façade of the Upson Brothers Grocery, in pen on blue paper. Even from a young age, Leila had a knack for doing what artists do best: interpreting their surroundings.

Leila's artistic inclinations continued to grow as she did. Like many in town, she attended nearby Lewis Academy. Her sixteenth birthday, which fell on Halloween 1900, was quite the event in Southington, complete with

Upson Brothers Grocery and the pen drawing Leila drew as a child.

a Halloween-themed party that her schoolmates, including Bradley Barnes, were eager to attend. After bobbing for apples and playing games, the evening concluded with Leila receiving a gold ring, a Halloween superstition that symbolizes a future betrothal. Ten years later, she married Bradley Barnes, who had been one of the guests at that evening's memorable party. Leila's love for nature extended beyond her art. She was an avid horticulturist, spending countless hours in the conservatory that Bradley had built for her and in the garden at 85 North Main Street. Her dedication to gardening was recognized in 1917 when she won a prize for the best house plant from the Southington Garden Club, an organization in which she was actively involved for many years. Leila often hosted garden tours and meetings at her home, showcasing her green thumb and artistic flair. She and Bradley shared a love for the outdoors, spending their summers at Block Island and Katahdin Lake in Maine at a resort known as the Big Houston Camp. In October 1915, Bradley and Leila attended the famous Astor Cup auto race at Sheepshead Bay, New York. Some of the wealthiest and most elite citizens were there to witness famous philanthropist Vincent Astor winning the prize cup. Bradley and Leila also enjoyed attending the theater, and the Barnes Museum boasts an impressive collection of Broadway playbills from the early 1900s. From the Follies to the Hippodrome, they saw it all together.

In 1927, Bradley and Leila purchased a summer home in Guilford, Connecticut, and named it Rock Edge. It was where Leila was at peace and found endless inspiration. She went to Rock Edge year-round, dedicating one of their cars by inscribing "Rock Edge" on the side of it. Her paintings from this period often depict schooners and ships navigating the restless sea, capturing the tranquility and majesty of the coastal landscape.

Oddly, Leila's diaries in the museum's collection span from 1935, when she was fifty-one, until her unexpected and untimely death at Rock Edge the age of sixty-eight in 1952. Bradley felt as if he had lost his best friend. The only personal note marking his wife's death is a line he wrote in his diary: "My all gone forever." Each of Leila's diaries in the collection is a "Line a Day," which are intended for just that, a single line each day for five years. These brief but daily entries reveal Leila's commitment to her friends, her small family (including their furry ones), to their charitable affairs and to her love of antiquing but mostly to improving her skills as an artist. In 1946, she frequently attended stencil classes in West Hartford, and her friendship with Hilma Johnson Black (1885–1949) played a significant role in developing her skills as an artist. Hilma, a fellow artist and close friend, often hosted Leila at her home in New Haven, where

Leila and Bradley in a boat with friends outside of Block Island.

Rockedge, located in Indian Cove in Guilford, Bradley and Leila's summer home.

One of the many seascapes Leila painted and displayed inside the home.

they spent time attending art classes at Yale for leisure, painting the same scene together and sharing ideas like painting Leila's dressing screen, which now resides in the Dressing Room in the museum. Leila painted various forms from her everyday life that inspired her. Today, paintings in the museum include numerous depictions of horses and ships. As her love of gardening flourished, most of her paintings are still-life depictions of flowers and garden bouquets, many of which came from her own hand and her own garden she shared with Bradley. Leila was actively involved in the Women's Auxiliary of the Bradley Memorial Hospital, overseeing several committees that benefited the public such as the Ways and Means Committee and the Counseling Committee. Leila was also on the board of the Women's Association of the First Congregational Church.

CHAPTER 5

ECHOES OF THE CIVIL WAR

I will fight till this Rebellion is put down or die in the ranks.[18]

A mong the most treasured artifacts in the Barnes Museum's archival collection are the writings, diaries and notes of Leila's grandfather Captain Andrew Upson. Andrew was born in 1825 to Levi (1795–1863) and Louisa (Todd) Upson (1788–1853) of Milldale, a small village in the southern area of Southington abutting the town of Cheshire. The Upson family owned a large farm in the area that prospered for many years. Andrew Upson firmly believed that one could be educated by books or through travel. Following his graduation from Yale College in 1845, he embarked on a brief teaching career that led him to Salem, New Jersey; Wellsboro, Pennsylvania; and Corning, New York, where he shared his passion for learning with his students. One of the earliest pieces in our collection from Upson is a detailed diary from 1848 chronicling his expedition following the Connecticut River northward from the state capital in Hartford through industrial Massachusetts, New Hampshire, Vermont and beyond. Through the pages of this diary, Andrew Upson offered a window into the social and economic threads that wove the tapestry of life in mid-nineteenth-century America. As he traversed New England by steamer train and his own two feet, he documented the landscapes he encountered—a bustling era of industrialization and societal transformation. Marveling at the industrial growth within the Connecticut River Valley, he witnessed the manufacturing prowess that dominated the time: "Massachusetts has always had a great reputation for enterprise, but one can form little opinion of her superiority until he has visited her works; then he will most surely award her all the glory that has ever been claimed." His eloquence in noting his admiration for the ingenuity of machinery was evident again as he noted, "It is truly wonderful to behold the achievements of human skill as exhibited in the variety and perfection of machinery."

In 1848, a journey from Southington, Connecticut, to Vermont was no small feat. Imagine bumping along in a carriage for several days, navigating rutted dirt roads and new rail lines that twisted through thick forests and over hilly terrain. The distance, roughly 180 miles, is a manageable road trip today, but back then it was a journey that required planning, patience and a bit of

Lieutenant Andrew Upson.

endurance. For someone from Connecticut, Vermont would have felt both remote and rugged, a place where the limited comforts felt in Southington were left behind in exchange for the wild beauty of the Green Mountains. Throughout his journey, Upson encountered both the splendor of New England's natural charm and the harsh realities of this new industrial age. From the beautiful vistas of Brattleboro to the rugged terrain near Bellows Falls, he experienced the full spectrum. When Upson visited the mills of Lowell, he quickly grasped the harsh realities of the time. He noticed the sharp contrast between wealth and poverty between what he witnessed there versus what he saw in Brattleboro: "The people here dress well, especially the young gents; and the taverns sell abundance of liquor...Brattleboro, I think rather surpasses any other place that I have yet visited in this respect." It was a sobering realization of how prosperity and destitution often coexisted, sometimes just a few miles apart. As he returned home, weary but enriched by his experiences, he reflected on the transformative power of travel: "I think my health has been improved by the journey very much & only regret that I did not devote the whole vacation to traveling." Upson's journey may have ended, but his thirst for knowledge and adventure continued to thrust him into new experiences.

Two years after his journey, he married Leila's grandmother Elizabeth Lewis Gridley (1827–1910) on April 18, 1850; together they purchased and ran a successful portion of the Upson farm in the Plantsville section of Southington. Elizabeth and Andrew had four children: Ida Maria (born 1853); Francis Root (born 1855), father of Leila Upson Barnes; William Calkins (born 1859); and Mary Brooks (born 1861). Upson made his views and opinion clear in his 1848 journal of his journey to the northern states in 1854. He put these beliefs into action by running and representing Southington in the Connecticut legislature. In 1854, the political landscape in the United States was chaotic, with the country grappling with issues that would eventually lead to the Civil War. This was a time when debates over enslavement and the economy were intensifying, especially with the passage of the Kansas-Nebraska Act on May 30, 1854. This act allowed the new settlers attempting to move into those territories and form governments to decide for themselves whether to allow for legal enslavement, effectively nullifying the Missouri Compromise, which had previously kept a balance between those states that practiced enslavement and those that did not. In response to these moral questions, the Republican Party formed in direct opposition to the expansion of forced captivity or enslavement in America. The political atmosphere was charged, and many, like Andrew Upson, felt compelled to take an active role in shaping the future of the nation. Serving in the Connecticut legislature in 1854, Upson was part of a broader movement of northerners who were increasingly concerned and taking action. Upson's involvement in politics during this time was driven by the urgent need to address the country's deepening divisions over enslavement and the direction in which the nation was heading— toward war:

> *They inquired if I voted for Lincoln "Yes & did my best to help elect him—I was a wide awake"—That made some staring—Finally one inquired if I would do the same again—"Certainly & more too"—"Would you enlist to fight us again?" "Yes, fight you till you get sick of rebellion"*
> *—May 20, 1863*

Upson's admission of being "Wide Awake" pays tribute to a group that supported Abraham Lincoln and opposed the proslavery factions in the country. The Wide Awakes were a group of young, enthusiastic Republicans who were particularly active during the 1860 presidential campaign. They supported Abraham Lincoln and the anti-enslavement platform of the Republican Party. The group was known for its marches, rallies and torchlight processions, all of which aimed to show their commitment to the Union and the abolitionist cause. In Connecticut on July 26, 1860,

Lincoln seated with his family, from a family member's photo album.

the Hartford Wide Awakes hosted the Newark, New Jersey Wide Awakes at a lavish banquet and rally at Hartford's city hall.[19] For someone like Andrew Upson, aligning with the Wide Awakes would have been a natural extension of his political beliefs, especially for someone involved in the Connecticut legislature during a period of such intense national debate. However, not everyone in Southington felt the same as the thirty-six-year-old Upson, as we witness in the museum's collection. Not everyone in Southington shared Upson's views, as we see in the museum's collection. Amon Bradley, a Democratic legislator, welcomed known Copperheads—northern Democrats who opposed the war and sympathized with the Confederacy—into his home, where they spoke with locals about a peaceful resolution. Amon had relatives in the South who were giving him firsthand accounts of the struggle there, but Upson felt that the pressure on the Union was justified. When the Civil War erupted, Andrew Upson enlisted in Company E of the Twentieth Connecticut Volunteers on July 21, 1862. His commission as a first lieutenant was confirmed on the same day. For some time, he worked to enlist as many from Southington as he could, and later during his service, he chronicled his experiences in letters to his beloved wife, Elizabeth, offering a detailed glimpse into the daily life of a Union soldier during the Civil War. One such entry from August 31, 1862, described the early morning hustle and bustle of camp life:

Camp Buckingham
Aug. 31ˢᵗ, 1862

My Dear Wife—

My first Sunday in camp has passed & I sit down to tell you something about it—We got up very early here—There is more or less noise through the night, corporals shouting for the next relief, the tramping of guards to and fro.…But an hour or so before sunrise the fellows begin to wake up—& tumble out—The consequence is a sleeper pretty surely gets waked and thinking it time for good soldiers to begin the day he dislikes to be behind—I have got up every morning long before sunrise—But probably before long I shall get so accustom to these as to sleep clear up to roll call.

Lieutenant Upson accounts compares this vivid early routine of rising before sunrise to the endless clamor of anxious military activity. Coming from remote Southington with a population of about three thousand people

Scan of a letter from
August 31, 1862.

in 1860, this would have been a stark contrast to the bustle he was used to: a farm with a humble house and several rumbustious young children. You can feel the contrast in these passages that not only provides insight into Lieutenant Upson's daily struggles in the war but also indicates what his life back home was like and his opinions on what he heard was happening here in town. Upson wrote home daily, if not twice daily, offering little bits of advice and encouragement to his wife from afar on how to run their farm and sustain her finances and food rations. As the war raged on, the delivery of mail in the United States faced severe disruptions, and sometimes their letters would take days if not weeks to get to each other; the anxiety this caused is felt several times throughout their correspondence. The conflict ravaged transportation infrastructure in most sections of the war-torn South, making it difficult for mail carriers to navigate through the chaos. Consequently, letters and packages experienced significant delays in reaching their intended recipients. Moreover, the scarcity of resources like clean clothing, drinking water, food and other supplies during wartime made for a desperate situation. For soldiers like Lieutenant Upson, access to money became a constant worry and challenge. The Civil War disrupted the economy, leading to inflation, shortages and the devaluation of money everywhere. Banks were strained, and many soldiers found themselves without regular access to money at all. In a letter dated April 23, 1863, Upson told Elizabeth how he wished he would receive some stamps soon. Stamps back then were more than just a way of sending letters—they became a form of currency, especially in areas where traditional money was hard to come by. Soldiers would use stamps to trade for goods or food, as they were a more reliable and portable means of exchange:

Stafford Co. House, Va.
April 23rd, 1863

My Dear Wife,

Yours of Saturday morning came in last evening—We are still here &
there is no new indications of moving—Had brigade drill yesterday &
this morning at 8½ I go on picket—It commenced raining during the night
& is coming down now as though the sea had got overhead—Once in a
while a drop falls on my paper—I am in fine spirits—& can do full duty
at meal times—Atwood & C.A. Roberts were sent to Washington 2 days
since Wiard arrived yesterday—Wish you would send me a few postage
stamps soon—Why do you wish to sell Bailey? The heifer is worth more
than 25 dollars—[Page 2] *The drums begin—I did not know it was so*
late—Must go—Shall write at length soon—

Yours Ever
A. Upson

The regiment did not see much action until the Battle of Chancellorsville,
Virginia, between April 30 and May 6, 1863. Just days before the battle,
Lieutenant Upson wrote a letter home to his wife from the Stafford
County House, a boardinghouse in Virginia about twenty miles north of
Chancellorsville. In the days leading up to the battle, there was a sense
of anticipation and unease among the commanders and soldiers. Both
the Union and Confederate armies were aware of each other's nearby
movements, and there were frequent skirmishes between scouting parties.
However, the exact timing and location of the impending battle were often
unclear. Military intelligence, reconnaissance efforts and communication
between commanding officers played crucial roles in determining the course
of events, evident in Upson's letter home on April 26, 1863:

There is no further news of operations in front—We shall know less of
actual transactions right here than you—The Washington papers for several
days have said just nothing about Hookers Army—Either news is scarce or
a close surveillance is maintained—I suppose you will try to keep yourself
uneasy—It is not necessary to worry, for we shall be as safe in one place as
another—Very likely we shall be shoved off one side somewhere to guard a
certain point & never see a reb. Nobody seems to feel much anxiety—any

way—we have learned to take things quite cool—That is the best way—
In fact here it is the only chance for rest or ease—We should eat our meals
& sleep even if a fight was imminent.

Despite some indications of an impending confrontation, the full scale
and intensity of the Battle of Chancellorsville were only fully realized once
the conflict unfolded. Mrs. Upson's cause for feeling "uneasy" was not
unfounded, as on April 30, Lieutenant Upson and his fellow soldiers found
themselves ambushed and thrust into battle. Upson's retelling of the conflict
reads like something out of one of today's war films, full of harrowing
moments that included taking the gun of a wounded soldier and dodging
whizzing bullets from the enemy. At one point, Upson found himself
completely alone in the field, bullets flying overhead. Running and hiding,
he ended his day burying his watch in the dirt next to the road, playing dead,
being robbed of his shoes, coat and jacket and ultimately being captured by
a "group of rebs."

In what has often been credited as Robert E. Lee's greatest victory of
the war, the battle had an approximate casualty total of more than 30,000
men, of which 17,000 were Union soldiers and 13,000 were Confederate.[20]
During the battle, Lieutenant Upson was taken prisoner and confined for
two weeks to the Confederate Libby Prison in
Richmond, Virginia. During the Civil War,
Libby Prison was considered one of the most
infamous Confederate prisons in Virginia.
It was initially a warehouse repurposed to
hold Union prisoners of war. The prison was
symbolic of the harsh conditions endured
by captives, as prisoners were subjected to
overcrowding, poor sanitation and inadequate
ventilation, which ultimately led to widespread
death and suffering. Due to the risk of severe
punishment if caught, escape attempts were
rare. Despite its grim reputation, Libby Prison
played a significant role in facilitating prisoner
exchanges between Union and Confederate
forces. Likely checking the papers daily for
news of her husband's condition, Elizabeth
Upson would have read the Wednesday May
13, 1863 *Hartford Courant*, which reported, "Of

A cabinet card featuring
Lieutenant Upson, taken during
his parole following his release
from the infamous Libby Prison.

the Union prisoners in the Libby prison, the higher officers are reserved, and all take their condition philosophically, looking forward to an exchange in a few days."[21] Lieutenant Upson's brief time there would have exposed him to these brutal conditions, leaving a lasting impression on the hardships of war.

After fourteen days in Libby Prison, Andrew Upson was released on May 14, 1863. A few short days later, while in transit, he wrote to his wife:

May 18, 1863

Moreover the Rebs have my note book and your photograph too. Don't get wrathy about it—They had me once, but not until I had given them many a bullet—Probably I could make out something of a report from the beginning of the movement down to the hour when our regiment retired from the entrenchment at Chancellorsville. Despite all hardship and vexations we kept jolly and judging from appearances our hearts were much more at ease than the Rebs. if they have got any—Our greatest trouble was to get anything to eat—We did not have so much as one good meal a day—I never lived on so little—We were exposed to the weather, which was bad from Tuesday P.M. till Thursday P.M. when we were put in a box car, very dirty and kept there 17 hours or until arriving in Richmond—After reaching the old Libby, while waiting to be examined a darky prisoner gave some two or three of us a bit of bread & bacon—I ate some of the bacon which was fat and somehow my stomach being empty it made one sick—The water too was very bad to drink and I got so weak that it was hard work to walk about the room—I eat very little while there—and when it was announced that we were to walk to City Point, 32 miles, it seemed an impossibility— But I was determined to try and once out in the air I felt refreshed and found my legs as good as any other officers—We left Richmond at 3 ½ P.M. Wednesday last. The purpose was not to halt at all until we had got to the end—But about 9 o'clock there came up a terrible thunder shower—It was so dark we could not see the road except by the flashes of lightning—We kept along in the rain and dark as well as possible.

After being released on parole, he found himself in a peculiar situation for an earnest soldier. Instead of being sent on leave or directed back to his company, he was stationed on furlough in Annapolis, Maryland. In his letters to Elizabeth, he detailed how himself and several others were required to check in every morning but then immediately dismissed, leaving him with nothing to do for the rest of the day but eagerly await mail and devour the latest news readings. During these idle moments, he longed even more acutely for his wife's companionship. On May 29, 1863, he asked Elizabeth to join him in Maryland, giving a flirtatious glimpse into their marriage: "One of the Germans, a major, has his duck of a wife here and another is expecting his every train—Don't know why Upson, though a Lt. should not have his too—We could spent a week or so happy as angels, such angels as we are." This request, clearly driven by a desire for a semblance of normalcy and companionship during the uncertainty of war following his imprisonment, shows that while much had changed since the Civil War, the need for family love was timeless. During the war, separation of soldier husbands from their wives inspired many wives to embark on the scary journey southward to visit their husbands stationed in Confederate territory. Travel was often fraught with danger, let alone from being a woman but also from disrupted train routes and the potential yet constant threat of nearby enemy forces. Despite these risks, it wasn't uncommon for soldiers to ask for visits from their loved ones, as they offered a brief respite from the harsh realities of the long war. However, not everyone could afford the luxury of this comfort, making it a rare and cherished opportunity. In his May 29, 1863 letter, Lieutenant Upson conveyed the perilous conditions to his wife while playfully requesting her to visit:

Annapolis, Md.
May 29ᵗʰ, 1863

If you come don't start with less than $50 nor much more and look out for pickpockets and sharpers—Writing paper and such things I can get here—Very likely you can buy a ticket clear through to Annapolis—At least from N.Y. without someone to look out for you I fear you might have trouble at New York—And yet you are a pretty cute Yankee—Put on a good face & go ahead.

In a letter to her husband mailed that same day, May 29, Elizabeth expressed her dismay at the spread of rumors fueled by Southington's Copperhead Democrats. These Copperheads, with their antiwar sentiments and often vitriolic rhetoric, sought to undermine the Union cause and sow discord among within their respective communities. Rumors were being spread throughout Southington that Upson was captured trying to *flee* the battle at Chancellorsville. The influence of local Copperheads extended beyond mere political opposition; they actively spread misinformation and propaganda to

INSULTING SOLDIERS.—Some miserable ignorant copperheads, under the training they obtain from their leaders, have come to regard it commendable and meritorious to insult and abuse soldiers from our army. An instance of this character which transpired near the City Hotel last Tuesday evening, came near raising a riot. Some thirty copperheads attacked some soldiers belonging to the 14th regiment, at home on a furlough. One soldier was knocked down, and had not the copperheads become alarmed at the appearance of numerous Union men, there would have been a disgraceful street fight. The soldiers conducted themselves with great forbearance, and seemed to have been completely by surprise, probably had not been at home long enough to learn that we have a few cowardly traitors here who deserve the halter, as richly as any in rebeldom. The police arrested three of these miscreants, but one or two were rescued by their friends. These men were not drank—it is a cool and preconcerted arrangement to maltreat and abuse those who have patriotically volunteered to risk their lives to save our liberties.

Copperhead newspaper article in the *Hartford Courant.*

Elizabeth Gridley Upson, Andrew's devoted wife and Leila's grandmother.

tarnish the reputations of Union soldiers like Lieutenant Upson. Despite facing such malicious accusations, Lieutenant Upson remained unbothered and urged his wife to disregard the divisive rhetoric of the Copperheads and instead focus on the truth of his experiences on the battlefield; hence he detailed in his many letters his experiences, from being robbed of everything on his person including his shoes to eventually being captured by Confederate soldiers. In his reply to her on June 1, 1863, he wrote, "But I know this spirit of Copperheadism is meaner than Satan himself & that it will torture every act so as to rob a man it hates of his just due—Don't you patronize a Copperhead in the least respect and much all their taunts and lies with open and brave defiance." As Elizabeth and Andrew Upson exchanged letters, they detailed the harsh realities and divisiveness of war and how it could change people. These more personal social challenges added another layer of strain to their already difficult situation. The battle wasn't just on the front lines, but also within the hearts and minds of their neighbors at home.

Despite all these anxieties, Elizabeth Upson did make the journey to see her husband, arriving on June 4, 1863, in Baltimore, where she stayed with him for about ten days until June 14, when she left on a steamboat from Alexandria, Virginia. We do not have any letters during this time, although we can imagine how good it must have been for them to spend that time together. Shortly after Elizabeth left Baltimore, Lieutenant Upson was called back to duty. He wrote to her from his camp on

June 15, 1863: "It is 8 o'clock P.M.; I am safely located in a room by myself and you in all probability are fast making distance homewards—Many a mile now separates us and we have to console ourselves upon recollections of the sweet past—The happy days have flown—happy to us two at least, for pretty much everything else was ignored by us except so far as it contributed to our comfort."

In July, Lieutenant Upson was called to take charge of about one hundred soldiers at Camp Abercrombie near Fort Ethan Allen in Arlington, Virginia. The group comprised former Union prisoners of war from nearly every branch in the military. He described the group in a letter to Elizabeth dated July 2, 1863: "It is made up convalescents who were to be sent to their regiments—They are from every regt. in the army and from every state in the union—I have artillery men, cavalry men, infantry men, in fact representations of every branch of the service—One of the fellows yesterday said it was the regt. of lost children—Some of them are good fellows and doubtless some are regular scamps—How we shall get along I can not say."

Lieutenant Upson's leadership skills and ability to handle a diverse group of soldiers at Camp Abercrombie didn't go unnoticed. Upson's steady hand and commitment to his duties set him apart. On October 23 of the same year, Andrew Upson was promoted to captain of Company K.[22] By this time, though, the Civil War had dragged on much longer than anyone had anticipated, leaving many fatigued and disheartened as it showed no signs of ending soon. Captain Upson wrote a Thanksgiving blessing to his family as he had the year before. Reporting from Fort Harker near Stevenson, Alabama, he had been stationed there for some time and continued to write home often. Fort Harker was vital during the campaign against Confederate General Braxton Bragg in Chattanooga, Tennessee, in July 1863, and the small town of Stevenson also served as a refugee camp and hospital following the battle. Occupation of the rail town ensured the Union-maintained control of supply lines in southeastern Tennessee and northeastern Alabama. In his own words, Captain Upson described seeing the refugees and their small children. He described seeing former enslaved African Americans eager to fight. Several of the sentiments he developed during his time around and in the camp were conveyed to his children in the letter:

November 18, 1863
Stevenson, Alabama
To Ida, Frank, Willie & Mary
My Dear Children,

I suppose this letter will arrive at its destination about Thanksgiving Day—Hoping it may add to your happiness on that occasion I sit up a few moments although it is time to go to bed and everyone around is asleep—Perhaps, children you do not understanding the real meaning of Thanksgiving Day—In the 1st place, you have enough to eat—that is, God has made the grain and fruits to grow during the past season, and so you have food—If now, there had been a scarcity of rain, or if war had prevailed around your home the crops would have failed—Down here there are many sections in which the corn was cut off for want of showers—In other sections it was all destroyed by the army—The people have scarcely nothing to eat—Papa has seen numbers of these people—Men, women and children—They had none of those good things that contribute to your comfort and for which you should give thanks to God—

In the 2d place, you have a snug and quiet home—In this part of the country families are often driven from their houses—They have to leave nearly everything and flee away to strange places—Often times women and their little ones are compelled to walk day and night—If the weather is cold or wet they suffer much and frequently become sick—You are not disturbed in this way and there is a reason why you should thank God who rules over all things—In the 3d place you have books, papers, schools and various privileges which thousands of children in other parts of the country know nothing about—It is a bad thing to grow up in ignorance—it is a bad thing to live where the people do not go to meeting or have good books and maps and the means of acquiring knowledge—God has case your lot where you have the benefit of almost every advantage to become learned and wise and useful—I hope you will so far understand this as to be thankful for your opportunities and not neglect them—

Now, my children, Thanksgiving Day is appointed that we may call to mind how much we owe to the Great and Good God—We are very apt to think too little of our common blessings—But if they are taken from us we begin to see their value—I hope you may never lose your schools, or your home, or the chance of enough to eat....I should like very much, Dear Children, to sit down with you at the Thanksgiving Supper—Perhaps another year God will permit us to meet on this anniversary—Whatever may be our condition let us be very thankful—Papa sends his best wishes and his tender affection to each of you and also to Mother and Grandmother—

From your loving father,
Andrew Upson

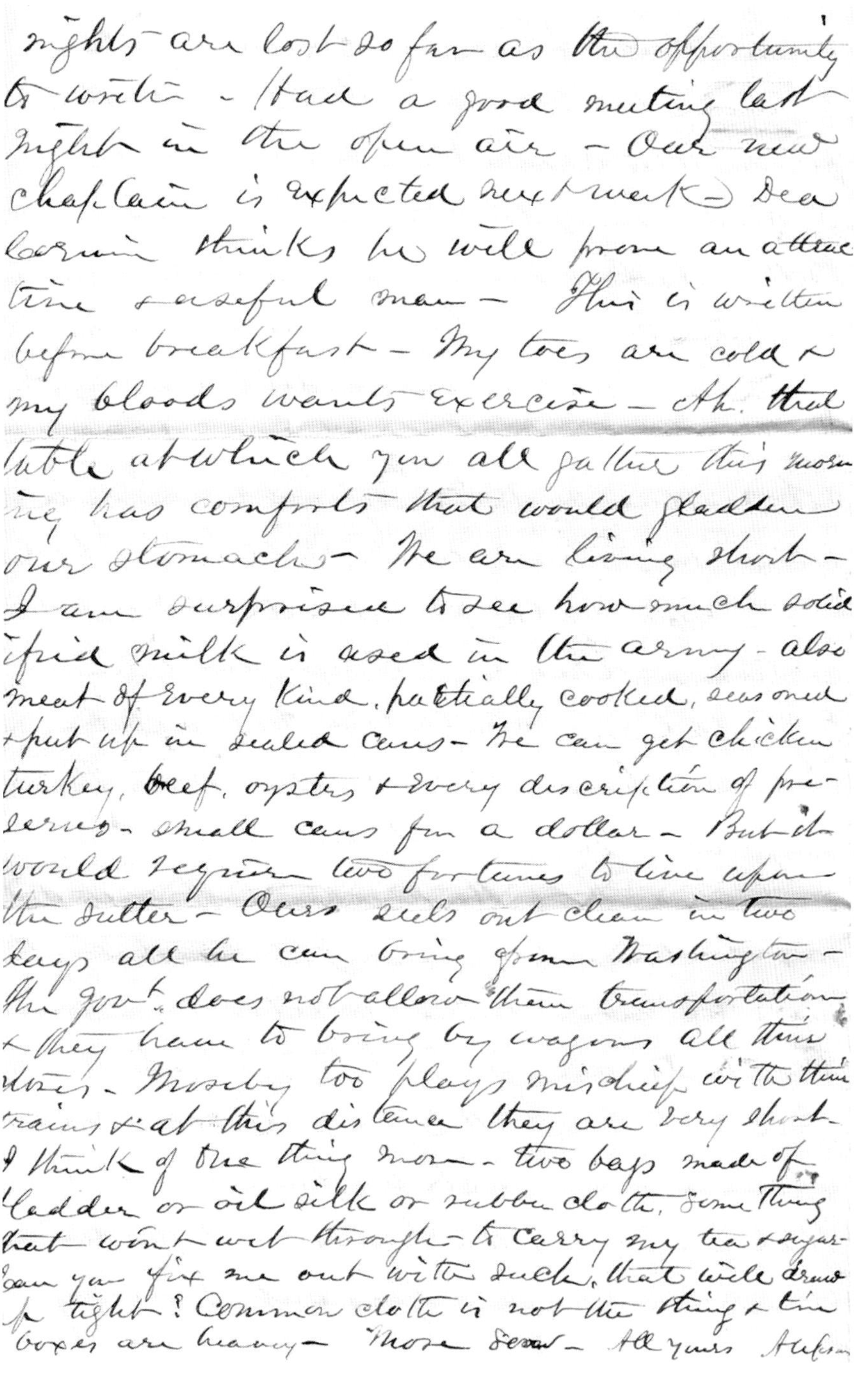
nights are lost so far as the opportunity
to write - Had a good meeting last
night in the open air - Our new
chaplain is expected next week - Dea
Cozzens thinks he will prove an attrac
tive & useful man - This is written
before breakfast - My toes are cold &
my bloods wants exercise - Ah. that
table at which you all gather this morn
ing has comforts that would gladden
our stomachs - We are living short -
I am surprised to see how much solid
ified milk is used in the army - also
meat of every kind, partially cooked, seasoned
& put up in sealed cans - We can get chicken
turkey, beef, oysters & every description of pre-
serves - small cans for a dollar - But it
would require two fortunes to live upon
the sutler - Ours sells out clean in two
days all he can bring from Washington -
The govt. does not allow them transportation
& they have to bring by wagons all their
stores - Mosby too plays mischief with their
trains & at this distance they are very short -
I think of one thing more - two bags made of
bladder or oil silk or rubber cloth, something
that won't wet through - to carry my tea & sugar -
Can you fix me out with such, that will draw
up tight? Common cloth is not the thing & tin
boxes are heavy - More soon - All yours Alpheus

Scan of a November 18, 1863 letter.

Frank R. Upson, Leila's father.

Unfortunately, Captain Upson would not make it home the following Thanksgiving. Less than two months after he wrote this letter, he died after succumbing to two gunshot wounds sustained during an ambush by Confederate soldiers in Tracy City, Tennessee, in early January 1864. Captain Upson was there with Company B of Connecticut's Twentieth Regiment to defend the rail line in Tracy City. The captain had been by the train depot with ten of his men when the ambush occurred. He was shot and captured along with several others and released after four hours. During his time recovering in the days following the incident, he continued to write home to his family. Word of mouth and local reporting indicated that the captain was feeling better, but several days later, he died on February 19, 1864. His body was returned home to Southington on February 29, 1864, and was interred at Southington's Quinnipiac Cemetery.

In an interesting twist of fate, Leila's grandfather Captain Andrew Upson was mentioned in several of her future mother-in-law Alice Bradley's diary entries. Although Alice's father, Amon, held views that aligned with Copperhead sentiments, the collection offers no evidence that he was an aggressor or extremist. Instead, what Alice's diary reveals is a mutual care for one of Southington's own, regardless of political party. On March 1, 1864, a fourteen-year-old Alice Bradley wrote in her diary, "March 1—I attended school as usual this forenoon; but this afternoon school did not keep as the funeral of Capt. Andrew Upson was to be attended at the church. Mother, sister, and myself attended the funeral. The church was very full. The flowers on the coffin were beautiful."

Captain Upson's sons, Frank and William, grew up to become successful grocers, opening the Upson Brothers Grocery Store on Center Street. In 1884, Frank's daughter, Leila Upson, was born, and she married Alice's son Bradley Barnes in 1910, intertwining the histories of these two Southington families. And the rest, as we say in the biz, is history.

CHAPTER 6

BRADLEY BARNES, SOUTHINGTON'S RICHEST MAN

O n February 28, 1919, Julia Arnold Bradley passed away at her home on North Main Street, where she had lived since the death of her husband, Franklin. Julia had remained an active and prominent figure in Southington, staying close to her brother-in-law, Norman, and her nephew Bradley Barnes. She was deeply involved in the community, notably as a founding member of Southington's Hannah Woodruff Chapter of the Daughters of the American Revolution, established in June 1897. A newspaper article from that time invited "all ladies eligible and desirous of organizing a local chapter" to gather at Julia's home. This meeting, set in one of the beautiful parlors of Julia's home, was much more than just a formal discussion; the clinking of teacups and the tinging of silver spoons would be secondary noise to the ladies exchanging stories of their grandfathers' and ancestors' service that tied them to our nation's founding. Under Julia's guidance as the first regent, the chapter quickly grew, boasting twenty-five members in its inaugural year. Julia's contributions to the community extended far beyond her involvement with the DAR. Even before her will was made public after her death, Julia had been actively giving back to Southington. Her husband, Franklin, had passed away years earlier, and their only son, Amon Edward Bradley, died unexpectedly in 1916. This series of personal losses, paired with the lack of a nearby quality hospital, motivated Julia to make a lasting impact on the town she had come to love very much.

Julia bequeathed nearly her entire estate, valued at around $225,000 in 1919 (a whopping approximate $3.7 million today), to establish Bradley

Julia Arnold Bradley portrait.

Memorial Hospital. Her will explicitly stated that the hospital was to serve the inhabitants of Southington and its surrounding areas, with a special focus on providing care for the sick and needy. Importantly, she insisted that the hospital operate without restrictions tied to any specific school of medicine or surgery, ensuring that it would be inclusive to all in its care for the community. After her passing, the board of trustees was formed to carry out her wishes, and her nephew, Bradley H. Barnes, played a key role as one of its members. It is important to note that Julia's decision to establish Bradley Memorial Hospital wasn't just a matter of public philanthropy—it was profoundly personal. After suffering the unimaginable loss of both her husband and son, she channeled her grief into something meaningful, ensuring that no other family would face a similar lack of emergency medical care in their most vulnerable moments.

Her actions took place against the backdrop of the Progressive era, a time when America was waking up to the need for social reform. This period, from the 1890s to the early 1920s, was marked by a collective effort to tackle the issues brought on by rapid industrialization and urban growth. Public health was a major focus, as access to medical care had been largely private and often out of reach for many. Julia's vision for a hospital that served everyone, regardless of background or circumstance, was a reflection of the era's spirit of compassion and progress. During the Progressive era, even small towns like Southington, which had a population of about 8,500 in 1920, were not immune to the social and economic shifts taking place across America. Although Southington was far from the bustling urban centers of Meriden and Waterbury, where these changes were most visible, the community still faced its own set of challenges. As industries grew and more people settled in town, the demand for better public health infrastructure became apparent. The push for Progressive era reforms was driven by the recognition that the traditional ways of life could no longer meet the demands of a rapidly evolving society, even in smaller communities like Southington. The need for accessible healthcare, improved living conditions, access to clean water and education became priorities, ensuring that everyone, regardless of where they lived, had access to the resources they needed for a healthier

Amon, Frank and Edward. Franklin and Edward would pass away before inheriting Amon's fortune.

life. Before the Progressive era, medicine in the United States was largely a private affair. Hospitals were often charity-based institutions funded by religious groups, and medical care was accessible mainly to the wealthy, who could afford private doctors. Public hospitals were few, and those that existed were typically underfunded and poorly equipped. Medical education was unregulated, leading to a wide variation in the quality of care provided. It was an interesting time to say the least. During the Progressive era, there was a shift in how society approached charity and public welfare. Instead of just offering direct aid, wealthy families were encouraged to fund institutions that would address the root causes of social issues. Julia Arnold Bradley's decision to fund Bradley Memorial Hospital was both a personal response to the losses in her life and a reflection of the Progressive era's push for public health reform. Even in a small town, there was a growing recognition that improving access to healthcare was crucial for the community's well-being, aligning with the broader movement of creating long-term solutions to social challenges.

On September 27, 1929, the *Meriden Daily Journal* noted that the Julia Bradley Hospital Corporation was close to securing a site for the hospital on the Haviland Property on Meriden Avenue. Julia's will stipulated the creation of a board of trustees to oversee the fund, with an executive committee that included notable Southington businessmen and residents Edwin S. Todd, Judge Thomas F. Welch, Paul B. Woodruff, James H. Pratt and Julia's nephew Bradley H. Barnes. Mr. Todd informed the papers that negotiations were

Image of Haviland Homestead, taken by Emerson Hazard, where BMH is today.

underway with Marion Pryor to purchase the corner of Meriden Avenue and Oakland Road, a four-and-a-half-acre property known for its high, flat landing that was ideal for the hospital building. The agreed-on price for the property was $14,500, a significant sum at the time. Much of the equity left by Julia was in insurance stocks inherited from her husband, Franklin, and from him by his father, Amon, likely dating back to the mid- to late 1800s. By the 1930s, these stocks had amassed a considerable amount and were valued at just over $750 apiece at the time, which would be about $16,000 to $17,000 today. It would take almost eighteen years to bring Julia's vision for a hospital here to fruition, but on October 1, 1940, Bradley Memorial Hospital officially opened its doors with three nurses and eight beds. Over time, the hospital expanded to include a maternity ward, a surgical wing and dental services. Although it merged with New Britain Hospital in 1995 to form the Hospital of Central Connecticut under Hartford Healthcare, Bradley Memorial continues to serve the community, albeit no longer as an inpatient facility. It now provides emergency and specialty services and continues to be a testament to Julia's enduring legacy of care and compassion for Southington.

Commemorative sign for the opening of Bradley Memorial Hospital.

Bradley's involvement with the formation of Bradley Memorial Hospital began in 1919 after the passing of his aunt, Julia, when he was thirty-six years old. Just eight years earlier, in March 1911, Bradley's father, Norman, passed away shortly after Bradley had moved into his newly renovated home with his wife, Leila, at 85 North Main Street. At the time of his death, Norman

Atwater Manufacturing staff, with Bradley pictured rear center.

was serving as president of Atwater Manufacturing Company located in nearby Plantsville Village in Southington. Atwater Manufacturing, founded in 1869 along the Farmington Canal and Quinnipiac River, was built on one of Southington's oldest industrial sites, where the town's first gristmill was established in 1767. The company specialized in producing carriage hardware and relied on a sixty-five-horsepower engine to supply steam power when water levels in the nearby river and retention pond were too low. Some of the original Atwater Manufacturing buildings on Atwater Street still stand and continue to serve manufacturing purposes today.

For many years, Atwater Manufacturing thrived under the leadership of Merrit Woodruff, who kept about one hundred people employed year-round. The company's goods were distributed nationwide, with a strong emphasis on expanding by selling predominately in the West. After Woodruff's tenure, Norman Barnes stepped in as president, steering the company through its shift from producing carriage hardware to crafting small bolts and parts during the rise of the automobile industry. Soon after Norman's takeover, Bradley's fascination with cars was born. For a young man like Bradley, whose family was involved in manufacturing parts that contributed to the production of vehicles, the allure of cars like the Model

T Ford or the luxury Packard was irresistible. This was a period when cars transitioned from being a luxury item for the wealthy to becoming more accessible to the public, thanks largely to innovations like the assembly line introduced by Henry Ford. This surge in demand required a vast supply of parts that at one time came from all over the country, including small bolts, nuts and other components made in Southington. It is worth noting again, as we often do during tours of the Barnes Museum, that Bradley was born in 1883, right at the dawn of the electrical age—an incredible time in history when electricity was just beginning to light up homes and revolutionize industries. Imagine growing up witnessing such rapid technological change. By 1910, Bradley's fascination with the latest technologies had grown, leading him naturally to wanting a car. His father, Norman, couldn't quite grasp why Bradley needed a car when he already had "one of the finest horses and hacks in town." But Norman's care for his son's interests won out, and he supported Bradley's decision but encouraged him to search for a new car with his Uncle Franklin Bradley, who Norman felt knew much more about the matter than he did.

Following his father's blessing, Bradley's enthusiasm kicked into high gear during a time when owning a car meant you were literally riding into the future. It's no wonder that he found himself corresponding with some of the top car manufacturers of the day, including the prestigious Packard Motor Car Company and the now lesser-known Pope Manufacturing Company. Pope Manufacturing Company, founded by Boston native Albert Augustus Pope in 1877, began as a bicycle manufacturer in Boston, Massachusetts, and Hartford, Connecticut. The company became famous for its Columbia brand bicycles, among some of the first to be mass-produced in the United States. Pope's ability to market his bicycles helped popularize cycling in America during the late nineteenth century, earning him the nickname "Father of the American Bicycle."[23] In the early teens, Pope shifted its focus to the automobile industry, bringing the Pope Manufacturing Company to Hartford. It produced a variety of vehicles, including electric cars and internal combustion engine models. The Pope-Hartford, one of its most successful lines, was built in Hartford from 1903 until 1914. These cars were known for their quality and luxury, appealing to the upper class and making Pope a well-known name in the early auto industry.

However, despite these early successes, Pope Manufacturing struggled to compete with companies like Ford, which utilized assembly line production to reduce costs. The company eventually faced financial difficulties, and by 1914, it had ceased automobile production. You can almost picture

Above: Bradley with horse and hack on the Town Green.

Left: Brad with his bicycle. All the cool kids his age had to have one!

Above: Bradley in his Pope-Hartford outside his homestead, the present Barnes Museum.

Left: AAA Ephemera commemorating Bradley's donation of the Pope.

Bradley, a young man with both the means and a deep love for this budding innovation, sitting at his desk at 85 North Main Street, writing letters to George Yule at Pope. That is exactly what he did, but he wasn't just asking for prices—Bradley was diving into details that really mattered to him and determined his purchasing choices, like horsepower, engine performance and even the quality of the leather seats. In each purchase that Bradley made, he was meticulous. From his goblets to his vehicles, he was a bit obsessed with getting the best product for his money. To him, the Pope wasn't just another car—it was an engineering marvel. George Yule, an executive at the Pope Manufacturing Company, described it as a "luxurious machine with graceful lines" in their exchanges. Fast-forward a bit, and Bradley's collection would include some truly remarkable cars, featuring models from a Franklin in 1918 and a Marmon in 1923, each with its own story and unique place in automotive history. However, of all the cars, the one that he cared for the most was his pride and joy: the 1912 Pope-Hartford Model 28 Roadster.

The Barnes Museum's papers offer a rare, personal look into the early days of the automobile industry, capturing not just the machines themselves but the passion with which they were owned and cherished. For Bradley Barnes, cars weren't just a means of transportation—they were a lifelong love affair. While many car enthusiasts of the 1920s, '30s and '40s eagerly traded in their old models for the latest innovation, Bradley recognized the value of what he had, and the Pope-Hartford was simply too good to let go. When Bradley Barnes passed away in 1973 at the age of ninety, he left the 1912 Pope Model 28 Roadster to AAA of New England. For more than fifty years, it has been proudly displayed within a glass-enclosed room at the AAA headquarters in West Hartford, Connecticut, although its future location is currently under consideration.

CHAPTER 7

A LEGACY IN GLASS

Leila was no stranger to Bradley's love of cars. In fact, one of the earliest photos we have of the couple shows Leila confidently behind the wheel of Bradley's car, donning an oversized hat and bundled against a chill. Bradley and Leila had been close friends since childhood, with Brad (as he was often called by Leila and friends) an annual guest at Leila's childhood Halloween-themed birthday parties when they were kids. This lifelong friendship naturally carried over into their marriage, where they shared and nurtured their passions—not just for cars but for animals, antique plates, gardening, mountain air and pressed glass goblets. From the moment they moved into their newly renovated home at 85 North Main Street in 1910, they embarked on a marriage that lasted more than forty years, a journey that blended Bradley's fascination with collectibles and history with Leila's love for nature and art. In the Barnes Museum collection, Leila's diaries begin in the 1930s and act as small windows into their shared daily life and the many moments that brought them joy. Most entries are brief but explain much, such as this one from March 1, 1935: "Brad's first sail with Frank Spencer," talking about their close connections with friends, of which they had many. Leila also recorded their frequent trips to their beloved cottage Rock Edge in Guilford, where they would spend many weekends on the water, tending to the garden, pruning roses and participating in community activities in Guilford. Leila was particularly fond of their ocean-side oasis and would note her trips down there often, as on May 11, 1935: "Indian Cove—to stay our first weekend."

Leila driving the car, circa 1912.

These were the years when Bradley and Leila truly got to enjoy each other's company. Bradley had stepped away from Atwater Manufacturing in 1930 after successfully negotiating the sale of the company. Bradley had stints in leadership at other companies in town, like the Aetna Nut Company, the Southington Hardware Company, Blakeslee Forging Company and Tubular Products Company. While he enjoyed these roles, it was Atwater he worked at the longest, from the time of his father's passing in 1911 until 1930; he served as vice-president, extending the company's life well beyond its original scope as a carriage hardware manufacturer. Retirement didn't mean that Bradley stopped working entirely. Far from it—he remained as busy as ever. Leila's diaries often noted his daily meetings and whereabouts, from the Hartford Auto Club to the YMCA, Bradley Memorial Hospital, the Southington Savings Bank (where he served as a trustee) and Southington Bank & Trust Company (where he was a charter member of the board of directors). This role mirrored a similar accomplishment of his grandfather Amon Bradley, who had secured the charter for the Southington Savings Bank himself in 1860.

Leila was deeply involved in the community here as well, and her days were full of balancing her responsibilities with a variety of activities that brought her joy. She was an active member of the Women's Auxiliary Group at the First Congregational Church, just steps away from their home, and when in Guilford, she was active with the Dorothy Whitfield Society. Each fall, Leila participated in the Southington Agricultural Fair, now known as the

Left: Leila and Brad at Rock Edge.

Below: The gardens as Bradley and Leila designed them in 1912.

The pergola, seen here, is still located on the grounds of the museum today.

Southington Apple Harvest Festival, where she served as a judge in the annual flower show and contest. Her passion for gardening extended into her art, with many of the paintings in our collection portraying flowers. Her love of flora extended into her active involvement with establishing the Southington Garden Club, which continues today as the Orchard Valley Garden Club.

The gardens at the Barnes Museum were a particular source of pride for both Bradley and Leila and was their favorite place to spend time together. They employed a full-time gardener, Peter Santagato (or Santago, 1886–1955), who was born in Caserta, Italy, and immigrated to America in 1903. Like many Italian immigrants coming to Southington for a better life in the late nineteenth and early twentieth centuries, Peter initially worked at Peck, Stow & Wilcox as a polisher before transitioning to full-time work as a gardener for the Barnes family in 1920. He remained with them until his passing in 1955, after which his son, Peter P. Santago (1922–2014), took over his father's role as caretaker of the grounds. Peter Sr. played a vital role in keeping the garden at the homestead beautiful, a relationship well documented in Leila's diaries. Leila meticulously noted every improvement Peter made, such as on March 25, 1944, when she wrote, "Peter did pergola and roses on wall," and a few weeks later on April 5 ("Peter spading garden"), followed by April 7 ("Indian Cove—Peter finished roses on wall"). Leila was also hands-on in selecting the plantings for their garden, working closely with Nicholas Grillo (1888–1975), a well-known Southington rose horticulturist and fellow Italian immigrant. Grillo is credited with developing the Thornless Beauty in 1938, the first hybrid tea rose without thorns—a beautiful and significant innovation during a time when hybrid tea roses were highly prized for their large flower heads and sweet fragrance. First Lady Eleanor Roosevelt was also a fan of the Grillo rose, ordering them for the White House. Grillo's greenhouse was located in the Marion village area of Southington and boasted many varieties, several of which Leila had planted in the garden at 85 North Main Street and at Rock Edge in Guilford. Leila and Bradley were committed to creating beautiful, lasting gardens.

Bradley and Leila shared a playful sense of humor, often exchanging holiday cards like many couples do. However, what made their exchanges even more delightful were the cards they sent from their pets. Bradley had a soft spot for animals, a trait that seemed to run in the Bradley-Barnes family. Each year on his birthday, Leila would send him a card from their family pet. One particularly endearing card was from their cat, Tags, with Leila affectionately addressing her husband as "Baddie." Tags wished Bradley a happy birthday for about eight years in a row. Their life together was defined by quiet dedication to their home, their hobbies and each other—a credo they lived by, encapsulated in the motto still displayed in their house today: "A world of strife shut out. A world of love shut in."

Bradley and Leila cherished the past and actively worked to preserve and celebrate it. The museum today remains much like they had it decorated and donned with their prized possessions. Most impressively remains the project they worked on together in 1941: the Goblet Room. The former conservatory remains today a kind of stained-glass window in and of itself. Depending on the time of day, the hundreds of individually different twinkling pressed glass goblets in the window of the former conservatory come together in a mosaic of early pressed glass manufacturing history. Nothing captured Bradley's attention over the course of several decades like his goblet collecting. Bradley's interest in this lesser-known form of art began in 1931, when glass collector and expert Ruth Webb Lee published her first book, *Handbook of Early American Pressed Glass Patterns*. Being an avid

Birthday card from Tags.

reader of antiques magazines, Bradley, who already possessed a decent collection of glass inherited through his home and ancestors, became intrigued in identifying the pieces in his own collection by using Lee's book. Ruth Webb Lee's early work on pattern or pressed glass had a huge impact on collectors of the time. She provided readers with detailed information about the patterns in their collections and encouraged them to seek out the complementary pieces in a patterned set or expand their collections with new acquisitions. Her books, such as *Handbook of Early American Pressed Glass Patterns*, became essential for enthusiasts like Bradley. It wasn't just Bradley; many people in the early 1900s were drawn to collecting, whether it was glassware, matchbooks or other items. (Bradley also collected matchbooks.) This was a period when collecting became a widespread and much-enjoyed hobby, driven by a growing interest in preserving the past and appreciating the craftsmanship of earlier eras.

Pressed glass, sometimes referred to as pattern glass or the "poor man's crystal," was produced in America between 1850 and 1910, with the peak of production hitting in the 1880s. It was produced during a time when craftsmanship went into the manufacture of everyday items to bring functionality and aesthetic to every table in America. During the nineteenth and early twentieth centuries, pressed glass was all the rage in England, the United States and Canada, with American factories leading the charge. Competition among manufacturers was fierce as they vied to create the most captivating patterns each year. Designs were meticulously crafted using cast-iron molds, subjected to intense heat before being carefully separated from the glass and allowed to cool. Pressed glass pieces typically exhibit two, three or four seams found at the base or along the sides, much like the glasses that are likely in your kitchen cabinet right now. While the number of seams doesn't necessarily indicate the age of a piece, smaller pieces used two-piece molds, while larger items like compotes or large pitchers required three-piece molds. Punch bowls, due to their size, often needed four-piece molds, as did square patterns that required more work to achieve their distinct shape. By the 1920s, pressed glass had fallen out of favor as crystal gained popularity, with affordable options imported from Europe and France flooding the market.

Mephistopheles goblet from the collection.

However, the economic downturn of the Great Depression led people back to pressed glass, often dubbed "Depression Glass," for its affordability and cheerful array of patterns and colors. Bradley strictly collected antique pressed glass goblets and was only interested in the ones manufactured during the rise of the industry between 1850 and 1910. Bradley enjoyed collecting different patterns that spanned a spectrum, including depictions of animals, fruits and florals. Examples in the Barnes Museum collection depict each of these but also include literary themes, including the rare 1875 Mephistopheles goblet based on the German folk demon found in the Faust legend. Within the collection of more than one thousand are about one hundred uranium-infused goblets. You read that correctly—uranium, the radioactive material used to produced atomic energy. Uranium was used to color pressed glass for many years and today is coveted by collectors for its eerie glow under a black light.

Glass enthusiasts and collectors were looking for everything from complete sets to finding each pattern of pressed glass goblets pictured in Lee's book. In fact, Bradley's collection of Lee's books and other publications identifying glass patterns contain small, penciled notations in Bradley's handwriting next to the patterns he already owned and a circle next the ones still desired.

By the early 1940s, Bradley was holding a steady correspondence with several antique and pressed glass goblet dealers, but it is Dudley R. Sibley (1895–1965) of West Hartford whom Bradley purchased most of his goblets from. Born in Providence, Rhode Island, Dudley lived in West Hartford for many years. Dudley worked for many years as director of the Hartford Better Business Bureau and as chairman of the First District Republican Committee of West Hartford.[24] Like Bradley, Mr. Sibley collected goblets as a hobby, interested in finding genuine originals dating the earliest days of pressed glass production in America—the 1840s. Like Bradley, collecting wasn't Mr. Sibley's primary profession. During regular hours, Sibley served as vice-president of the Automobile Insurance Company of Hartford. After seeing one of Sibley's ads in an antique magazine, Bradley made his first purchase from Mr. Sibley on March 15, 1943. In June and July 1943, Bradley purchased more than thirty goblets for $350, equivalent to approximately $5,700 today. In a letter to Sibley on March 22, 1943, Bradley disclosed, "I have been collecting a little over two years and now have somewhere around 400 of them. I find that it an extremely interesting hobby, much more than I thought it would be when I first started." Glass collecting as a hobby involves a lot of homework, persistence and patience. You may think that you have a handle on the name of a specific pattern and then another name for the same pattern appears. Examples are the Hobnail pattern, which is also sometimes referred to as Thousand Eye. Ruby Thumbprint is more commonly known as Kings Crown. Although there are no figures to show exactly how many patterns were produced by American glassmakers during its peak in the late nineteenth century, several reference books have noted that there are likely hundreds of patterns and variations of the original patterns. Some of the rarest pieces in Bradley's collection remain unidentified, and we encourage a crowdsourcing effort as we continue to re-identify and catalogue the goblet collection.

In 1941 alone, Leila noted in her diary the purchase of 188 goblets from auctions and antique shops across the state. Leila enjoyed collecting the goblets too and often picked them up for her husband when she saw them. On May 6, 1941, Leila wrote, "Glass shelves put up in Conservatory & Goblets arranged"—a humble entry that barely touches the work that went into making the Goblet Room what it is today. When Leila began placing the goblets in the conservatory, she kept a meticulous record of each one they owned at the time noting the pattern name, how much it cost and where they purchased it from. This continues to be a primary source for us today as the Barnes Museum began a catalogue and identification project in 2021

A snapshot of the Goblet Room inside the museum.

that aims to identify the current pattern name and create an online index of the goblet collection. Bradley and Leila continued collecting goblets for many years. Today, the Barnes Museum displays more than five hundred on a daily basis, with another five hundred or so in storage. It remains one of the largest collections in the country and is a peaceful reprieve within the museum for staff and guests alike.

THE BEQUEATHAL AND ITS IMPACT

When Leila unexpectedly passed away on October 10, 1952, just twenty days shy of her sixty-ninth birthday, Bradley was devastated. He had lost his lifelong companion and best friend. In her diary, he wrote the final entry for that year: "End of the world. My all gone forever." Less than ten years after her death, Bradley stopped visiting their Guilford home, unable to bear revisiting the place that had meant so much to his wife and where she had passed away. For many years, lore at the Barnes Museum held that Bradley shut off Leila's room on the second floor of their home, preserving it exactly as she left it in her final days. While nothing in the collection confirms this, today, when you visit Leila's bedroom, filled with her paintings, drawers overflowing with her dresses and paintbrushes abandoned from her last unfinished project, you feel as if she is still there. Her personal touches are everywhere—from her dressing room, designed as every girl's dream closet, to the countless hat boxes, shoe boxes and receipts from her favorite department store, the famous G. Fox & Company of Hartford. At the age of sixty-nine, Bradley found himself alone in Southington for the first time in his life. All his other family members had long since passed away, and although he maintained correspondence and sent Christmas letters with money to those he was fond of, his life was never the same after Leila's death.

There are many members of the Southington community alive today who recall seeing Mr. Barnes walking back home from bank meetings, driving around in his Pope or sitting on the front porch of his home, watching the cars go by on North Main Street. In 1955, at the age of seventy-two, he was awarded the Unico Gold Medal Award from the community for his dedication to Bradley Memorial Hospital as a trustee and for his role in establishing and maintaining stock in the Southington Country Club. Despite his age, he remained actively involved as a member of the board of directors for the Oak Hill Cemetery Association and generously supported the YMCA, where he served for many years on their board. That same year, Bradley was still the owner of Rock Edge and was actively participating in the formation of the Indian Cove Improvement Association

Bradley Barnes enjoying his garden and feeding a squirrel.

in Guilford, where he also served on the Finance Committee. Over the next ten years, as his health began to decline, Bradley gradually stepped back from many of his responsibilities. By the latter half of the 1960s, he required the use of a wheelchair and spent most of his time in the lower levels of his home at 85 North Main Street. His bedroom was moved to the den, and his nurses, Betty LeFay (1931–2000) and Barbara Ball (1927–1997), often brought him outside to enjoy the garden. Even in his later years, the simple pleasures he had always enjoyed in life brought him joy—he loved sitting in the garden, watching the animals and feeding the squirrels and the barn cat.

From his perch at 85 North Main Street, Bradley witnessed Southington transform before his eyes. The once quiet rural town, with its rolling fields of farmland, began to shift into a suburban outlet. He saw the construction of Interstate 84, a highway that sliced through Southington and connected Waterbury to Hartford, marking the beginning of a new era for the town. Bradley also watched as the downtown area outside his window changed— the Woodruff property across the street was repurposed into the YMCA, and houses adjacent to his property were torn down to make way for storefronts and businesses. Next to him, the Colonial Theatre bustled with activity; Bradley enjoyed attending movies there, a tradition he maintained even after Leila's passing. He continued to visit the theater once a week, right up until his death on February 23, 1973, just a month after celebrating his ninetieth birthday. Bradley's passing in 1973 raised numerous questions in the community, much like the ones left behind by his grandfather Amon Bradley in 1906. His extensive property holdings, both adjacent to his home and throughout Southington, contributed to an estate that the press

Bradley's nurse Barbara. Bradley left her $100,000 in his will.

described as "one of the largest ever" in town. Adjusted for inflation, his 1973 estate would be worth more than $20 million today—a considerable fortune by any standard. Bradley was meticulous in how he allocated his wealth. He appointed the Southington Bank and Trust Company as the executor of his will, ensuring that his bequests were carried out with precision. Rock Edge, his Guilford home, was left to its longtime caretaker, Allen Roberts, along with $25,000 for its upkeep. Significant sums were also willed to organizations close to his heart, such as $20,000 to the Oak Hill Cemetery Association and $15,000 to the Quinnipiac Cemetery Association Fund. His generosity extended to his staff, with $75,000 left to his homestead caretaker, Peter Santago, and $5,000 in memory of Peter's father. Each of his nurses, Betty and Barbara, received $100,000—a sum equivalent to about $750,000 today.

Bradley's generosity extended to nearly thirty individuals, including other nurses, distant relatives and local residents, with bequests ranging from $1,000 to $25,000. Numerous organizations also benefited, including the Southington YMCA across the street, which received $75,000; the Newington Home for Crippled Children, $10,000; the Connecticut Humane Society, $5,000; the First Baptist Church of Southington, $20,000; the First Congregational Church of Southington, $20,000; Christ Episcopal Church of Guilford, $5,000; the Guilford Public Library, $5,000; and Gaylord Hospital and Sanatorium of Wallingford, $10,000. What truly stands out is how Bradley chose to preserve his family's legacy in Southington. Arguably the most precious bequeathal was his entire residence at 85 North Main Street to the Town of Southington. Every item—from photographs and tableware to wall hangings and light switches—remained as he left it. His will stipulated that the property was to be used as a museum and historical library or for "such other historical, cultural, and artistic purposes as deemed desirable by the library board." Bradley had also left to the town $10,000 for the board of education and $10,000 to the Southington Public Library.

The gift of the homestead and all of its contents sent residents into a frenzy, and for months they debated accepting the house and turning it into a museum. What helped was the fact that Bradley had set up a $200,000 trust "for the purpose of maintaining, repairing, improving, and insuring the homestead and real estate." In June 1973, the Southington Town Council was debating accepting Bradley's gift, weighing the cost it would take to bring the then 140-year-old homestead into the 1970s. Emergency door, HVAC upgrades and all the things the homestead required to become a museum seemed like a steep hill for them to climb. A co-executor of the estate from the Southington Bank & Trust Company appealed to the council, stating, "[I]t was never his intention to make an offer we could not refuse because to Mr. Barnes, the unappreciated gift and unwanted gift is an empty gift without lasting benefit to either the giver or the receiver."

The year 1973 was an interesting time for the board of directors of the Southington Public Library, as its members were engaged in a familiar task, one they would revisit fifty years later in 2023: planning for the construction of a new Southington Public Library. The twenty-one-thousand-square-foot facility was slated to be built on the site of the former South Center School. The focus shifted significantly when the board was unexpectedly tasked with managing Bradley Barnes's bequest of his homestead. This surprise gift required the board to quickly pivot, developing reports on the cost of operations to the town council and conducting analyses on the viability of turning the homestead into a museum. Throughout the months following Bradley's passing in January until the middle of summer 1973, much of the discussion centered on persuading the town council to take on this significant and historically important responsibility. To navigate the entire process, the board of directors appointed Milton J. Wooding (1911–1995), the former chairman of the board of library directors, as the executive director of the Barnes Museum. Milton's job was so much more, as he was not only tasked with being the liaison between the library board and the council, but he was also charged with the challenging task of transforming Bradley Barnes's home into a municipal museum. Milton Wooding's daily efforts at the homestead were for a time conducted alongside caretaker Peter Santago, whose knowledge of Mr. Barnes helped Milton contextualize and sort through the vast collection Bradley had kept and collected over the years. He began by cataloguing the entire museum on index cards, writing each item in the collection and expanding on the context of the item over time. Like many at the age of ninety, Bradley was inactive and had kept much of his newspapers in stacks in his office, which resembled something of a maze by the time Milton walked in to make sense of it all.

The Barnes house — an unwanted gift?

It's been more than three months now since the will of the late Bradley H. Barnes of Southington was made public and citizens of that town learned that they had been left the Bradley homestead on North Main St. — if they wanted it.

The Town of Southington, or more specifically, the Town Council and the Board of Library Directors, is still trying to decide whether to accept the gift.

The Barnes house, a fine old structure surrounded by parklike grounds, is located at the northern end of Southington Center and would have been the logical place to end commercial zoning except that zoning officials have already skipped by it to permit business offices farther up the street.

But at any rate the grounds of the Barnes estate are like an oasis in the business area and might be expected to remain that way if the town took possession of them.

Mr. Barnes, an industrialist who died earlier his year at the age of 90, specified that the property be used as a historical library and museum and that it be maintained by the Board of Library Directors.

He backed up this gift with a $200,000 trust fund. The income from this fund — an estimated $8,-000 to $10,000 a year — would be used toward maintenance of the property. Total maintenance and operating costs, it has been estimated, would be annually more than twice this amount.

Nevertheless, it would seem that the Barnes bequest was an exceedingly generous one and one which the Town of Southington could scarcely refuse.

Council Chairman John Daley last week expressed some pardonable annoyance with the Board of Library Directors because the board still — after three months — has not prepared a report on what it proposes to do with the bequest.

It would seem that it's time for a decision, one way or the other. If the town doesn't want the property, it will go to Bradley Memorial Hospital.

As a co-executor of the Barnes estate put it to town officials recently, ". . . . it was never his intent to make an offer we could not refuse, because, to Mr. Barnes, the unappreciated gift and unwanted gift is an empty gift without lasting benefit to either the giver or the receiver."

Left: The Barnes Museum was recalled by some as an unwanted gift.

Below: Milton Wooding outside the Barnes in 1974.

Milton also played a crucial role in managing the financial aspects of the museum's transition. The town provided a modest annual income to support museum operations, covering the essential time and effort needed to ready the homestead for public display while preserving its historical integrity. However, the vastness of the collection (excluding the goblets) made progress slow. The town council required detailed reports and assurances before fully committing to the project, leading to several proposals and debates about the museum's operation and management. Ultimately, a compromise was reached that granted control to the library board, in line with Bradley's wishes, while also encouraging collaboration with the Southington Historical Society to showcase historical objects and programs. In February 1974, after months of cataloguing, cleaning and preparing the house for its new role as a museum, Wooding submitted a budget request of approximately $22,000. This included $1,200 for utilities like gas, electric, water and telephone services and $5,900 for maintenance of the house and grounds, which encompassed upgrades such as interior painting, tree removal and other necessary materials. The trust established by Bradley provided $9,000 of the requested funds, leaving the remainder to be covered by the town. Once approved, Wooding worked tirelessly, about eight hours a day without pay, to ready the museum for its planned opening in the fall of 1974. He received significant support from his wife, Helen; his brother, James; and his son, Phil, during this period. On December 7, 1974, the museum opened its doors to a select group of privately invited guests, offering them a cherished opportunity to tour one of Southington's grandest homesteads. Following the private opening, the museum became available for public tours by private appointment on Tuesdays, Thursdays and Saturdays, accommodating four guests at a time.

THE BARNES MUSEUM'S FIRST INTERN: RAYMOND SMITH

In the summer of 1973, Raymond Smith, a Yale student pursuing a doctoral degree in American Studies, was exploring an antiques shop in New Haven when he came across a remarkable collection of glass plate negatives. His research primarily focused on the late nineteenth and early twentieth centuries, a transformative period for photography in the nation. He spent months attempting to identify these rare turn-of-the-

Emerson Hazard family photo.

century photographs. Ray was able to trace the source of the negatives to Southington and came to town seeking to find out more. He was quickly directed to the door of 85 North Main Street, where he was told a remarkable collection of early editions of *Southington Weekly Phoenix* resided, some as early as 1875. Smith asked Mr. Wooding if he could volunteer with him at the museum, work for free as an intern and research the collection. During his time at the museum, Ray made some fascinating discoveries about Southington's history, particularly identifying the photographer behind a significant number of images of the Bradley and Barnes families: Emerson W. Hazard (1854–1926). Recognizing the fragile state of the newspapers he encountered, Smith collaborated with Yale University and the Wisconsin Historical Society to spearhead efforts to microfilm a portion of the surviving issues. In fact, during my second summer at the museum, I came across some of Smith's work in the attic—a large, flat cardboard box containing copies of the *Southington Phoenix*, with "Please keep flat—Ray" scrawled across the top in large handwriting.

Smith's work on Emerson Hazard is commendable, and he often published his findings in local papers and gave talks about photography at the historical society exploring Hazard's work experimenting with photography styles and different equipment. Hazard was a prominent photographer for this area of Connecticut, known for capturing the everyday life of working-class citizens sometimes from the wheels of his bicycle. Born in nearby Waterbury, Hazard eventually settled in Southington, where he operated a photography studio at the corner of Main Street and Berlin Avenue from around 1885 to 1898. His studio work was well regarded, and for many years, the Bradley-Barnes families exclusively visited Hazard for their portraits. Hazard was also deeply involved in the local community, contributing to exhibitions like the Southington Agricultural Fair and gifting residents' portraits of their homes. After closing his studio in 1898, he continued as a freelance photographer, focusing on landscapes and occasional portraits. His legacy in Southington

Photo of the house on Oak Street, taken by Emerson Hazard.

Ray Smith self-portrait, taken in 1975.

is preserved through his photographs, many of which are marked with his logo on cabinet cards or with his handwriting on glass plates.

In February 2022, the Barnes Museum became the recipient of more than one hundred glass plate negatives—those very same negatives that Ray discovered in New Haven in 1973. This generous gift came from the estate of Raymond Smith, who passed away on December 30, 2021, at the age of eighty-four. For many years, Smith owned R.W. Smith Books in New Haven, where he dealt in antique books and publications. It was his wish that after his passing the Barnes Museum would accept the glass plate negatives and the extensive research he conducted for his thesis during his time here. Smith's contributions not only deepened our understanding of Southington's past but also shed new light on the Bradley family's place in Southington's history.

Reflecting on the legacy of the Barnes Museum, it's clear that this place has grown beyond being just a collection of artifacts and memories. It's become a living testament to Southington's history and to the people who played a role in shaping it—from Bradley Barnes's careful curation of items to Raymond Smith's dedicated research. Every artifact, photograph and document within these walls tells its own story, and these stories continue to grow with each new discovery and each generation that walks through the door. The Barnes Museum stands as a beacon for anyone wanting to connect with the past, preserving Southington's heritage for years to come. Closing this chapter, we're reminded that the Barnes Museum isn't just about what's been—it's about what's yet to come, as the journey of preservation, education and discovery continues.

NOTES

Chapter 1

1. Timlow, *Ecclesiastical and Other Sketches of Southington*, 62.
2. State of Connecticut, *Public Records of the Colony of Connecticut*.
3. Bradley, *Descendants of Isaac Bradley*, 128.
4. Green, *Eli Whitney and the Birth of American Technology*.
5. Le Blanc, *Short History of the U.S. Working Class*.
6. Steiner, *History of Slavery in Connecticut*.
7. Cedrone, "Everyman's Time."
8. Jaffee, *New Nation of Goods*, 182.
9. New England tin peddling began in Berlin, Connecticut, in the late eighteenth century with an Irish descendent named William Pattison. The Bradley Homestead in Southington is on the boarder of Berlin. Rainer, "'Sharper' Image," 28.
10. National Endowment for the Humanities, "Litchfield Enquirer. [Volume] (Litchfield, Conn.) 1829–Current."

Chapter 2

11. The company formed noting that the "name may sue and be sued, may hold property not exceeding five hundred dollars in amount; and shall have power to fill vacancies by voluntary enlistment; to appoint such officers as they may deem

necessary or expedient; to make by-laws not inconsistent with the laws of this state…provided that no member of said company shall be excused from his poll tax, nor be exempt from military duty until an engine is procured for the use of said company: nor shall at any time, more than twenty-five persons be exempt aforesaid." State of Connecticut, *Private and Special Laws of the State*, 583.

12. *Evening Post*, April 30, 1842, 2.
13. Federal Writers' Project for the State of Connecticut, *Connecticut*.
14. Henry was the son of Roswell, Amon's older brother. He graduated from Yale in 1853 and soon after came to Southington. Well respected, he held the position of town clerk, treasurer, registrar and judge of probate. In 1859, he represented Southington in the House of Representatives. According to Timlow in his *Ecclesiastical History of Southington*, he was sensitive but kind, and although he suffered from a physical ailment that ultimately claimed his life, he touched the lives of many while he was alive. Yale University, Class of 1853, 37.
15. U.S. Census, 1880, "Francis Dyer."
16. We often say at the museum that the Bradleys were a big fish in their respective pond. Chernow, *House of Morgan*, 42.
17. *American Cutler*.

Chapter 5

18. Storrs, *"Twentieth Connecticut,"* 236.
19. Grinspan, *Wide Awake*.
20. American Battlefield Trust, "Chancellorsville."
21. *Hartford Courant*, May 12, 1863, 3.
22. Ancestry.com, "U.S., Civil War Soldier Records and Profiles, 1861–1865.

Chapter 6

23. Goddard, *Colonel Albert Pope*.

Chapter 7

24. *Hartford Courant,* June 14, 1965, 2.

BIBLIOGRAPHY

Chapter 1

Bradley, Leonard Abram. *Descendants of Isaac Bradley of Branford and East Haven, Connecticut, 1650–1898: Together with a Brief History of the Various Bradley Families in New England.* N.p.: privately printed, 1917.

Cedrone, Sarajane. "Everyman's Time: The Rise and Fall of Connecticut Clockmaking." Connecticut Explored, January 13, 2016. https://www.ctexplored.org/everymans-time-the-rise-and-fall-of-connecticut-clockmaking.

Green, Constance McLaughlin. *Eli Whitney and the Birth of American Technology.* Boston: Little, Brown, 1956.

Jaffee, David. *A New Nation of Goods: The Material Culture of Early America.* Philadelphia: University of Pennsylvania Press, 2010.

Le Blanc, Paul. *A Short History of the U.S. Working Class: From Colonial Times to the Twenty-First Century.* Chicago, IL: Haymarket Books, 2017.

National Endowment for the Humanities. "*Litchfield Enquirer.* [Volume] (Litchfield, Conn.) 1829–Current, January 21, 1847, Image 2." January 21, 1847. https://chroniclingamerica.loc.gov/lccn/sn84020071/1847-01-21/ed-1/seq-2.

The Public Records of the Colony of Connecticut [1636–1776]…: *1757–1762.* Press of the Case, 1880.

Rainer, Joseph T. "The 'Sharper' Image: Yankee Peddlers, Southern Consumers, and the Market Revolution." *Business and Economic History* 26, no. 1 (1997): 27–44. http://www.jstor.org/stable/23703298.

Steiner, Bernard Christian. *History of Slavery in Connecticut*. Baltimore, MD: Johns Hopkins University Press, 1893. http://archive.org/details/histslaveryconn00steirich.

Timlow, Heman Rowlee. *Ecclesiastical and Other Sketches of Southington, Conn.* Hartford, CT: Case, Lockwood and Brainard Company, 1875.

Chapter 2

The American Cutler, Official Organ of the Cutlery Industry: A Monthly Publication Devoted to the American Cutlery Trade…. New York: Cutlery Publishing Company, 1921.

Chernow, Ron. *The House of Morgan: An American Banking Dynasty and the Rise of Modern Finance*. New York: Grove/Atlantic Inc., 2010.

Evening Post. April 30, 1842. Accessed March 1, 2024. https://www.newspapers.com/image/32114810.

Federal Writers' Project for the State of Connecticut. *Connecticut: A Guide to Its Roads, Lore, and People*. Boston: Houghton Mifflin, 1938.

Private and Special Laws of the State of Connecticut. State of Connecticut, 1837. Available on Google Books, or the CT Digital Archive.

U.S. Census, 1880. "Francis Dyer." 73a (roll 99). National Archives and Records Administration, 1880. https://www.ancestry.com/discoveryui-content/view/16928420:6742.

Yale University, Class of 1853. New Haven, Connecticut, Pamphlet Box, 1860.

Chapter 5

American Battlefield Trust. "Chancellorsville." https://www.battlefields.org/learn/civil-war/battles/chancellorsville.

American Industries. Washington, D.C.: National Association of Manufacturers, 1924.

Ancestry.com. "U.S., Civil War Soldier Records and Profiles, 1861–1865." Accessed February 26, 2024. https://www.ancestry.com.

Grinspan, Jon. *Wide Awake: The Forgotten Force that Elected Lincoln and Spurred the Civil War*. New York: Bloomsbury Publishing USA, 2024.

Hartford Courant. May 12, 1863. Accessed April 11, 2024. https://www.newspapers.com/image/369182250.

Storrs, John Whiting. *The "Twentieth Connecticut": A Regimental History*. Waterbury, CT: Press of the *Naugatuck Valley Sentinel*, 1886.

General Bibliography

Aetna Insurance Company Records. UConn Archives & Special Collections. Accessed March 1, 2024. https://archivessearch.lib.uconn.edu/repositories/2/resources/1189.

American Battlefield Trust. "Chancellorsville." Accessed February 26, 2024. https://www.battlefields.org/learn/civil-war/battles/chancellorsville.

American Industries. N.p.: National Association of Manufacturers, 1924.

Ancestry.com. "Connecticut, U.S., Town Marriage Records, Pre-1870 (Barbour Collection)." Accessed March 1, 2024. https://www.ancestry.com/discoveryui-content/view/124563:1062?tid=&pid=&queryId=4432b4f3-7ae7-4f1e-915d-052f9e142f58&_phsrc=XqX305&_phstart=successSource.

———. "Connecticut, U.S., Wills and Probate Records, 1609–1999." Accessed February 26, 2024. https://www.ancestry.com/discoveryui-content/view/245 1852:9049?tid=&pid=&queryId=4f6da297-4d67-4d63-8380-38c20c8360cc&_phsrc=XqX216&_phstart=successSource.

———. "Pietro Santagato (Santago)*?—Facts." Accessed April 30, 2024. https://www.ancestry.com/family-tree/person/tree/157249541/person/272407419773/facts.

———. "U.S., Civil War Soldier Records and Profiles, 1861–1865." Accessed February 26, 2024. https://www.ancestry.com/discoveryui-content/view/810 699:1555?tid=&pid=&queryId=b4a0fdc0-6291-4429-a7a7-728c1de1f740&_phsrc=XqX235&_phstart=successSource.

Applegate, Edd. "The Earliest Collegiate Schools of Business in the United States." n.d. ERIC (Education Resources Information Center).

Benham, J.H. *1875 New Haven CT Directory*. 1875. http://archive.org/details/1875 NewHavenCTDirectoryConnecticut.

Bradley, Leonard Abram. *Descendants of Isaac Bradley of Branford and East Haven, Connecticut, 1650–1898: Together with a Brief History of the Various Bradley Families in New England*. N.p.: privately printed, 1917.

Chernow, Ron. *The House of Morgan: An American Banking Dynasty and the Rise of Modern Finance*. New York: Grove Atlantic Inc., 2010.

Connecticut Daughters of the American Revolution. *Chapter Sketches, Connecticut Daughters of the American Revolution; Patron Saints*. Edited by Mary Philotheta Root, Connecticut Chapters of the Daughters of the American Revolution, New Haven, 1901. Available at the Library of Congress, loc.gov, and Internet Archive, archive.org.

Connecticut Daughters of the American Revolution, and Emilie M. Mouat. *Connecticut State History of the Daughters of the American Revolution*. (Hartford)

Connecticut Daughters of the American Revolution, 1929. http://archive.org/details/connecticutstate00conn_0.

Connecticut General Assembly. *Roll of State Officers and Members of General Assembly of Connecticut, from 1776 to 1881 : With an Appendix Giving the Congressional Delegates, Judges of the Supreme and Superior Courts, and the Date of Incorporation of the Cities, Boroughs, and Towns.* Hartford, CT: Press of the Case, Lockwood & Brainard Company, 1881. http://archive.org/details/rollofstateoffic00conn_0.

Cowden, Joanna D. "The Politics of Dissent: Civil War Democrats in Connecticut." *New England Quarterly* 56, no. 4 (1983): 538–54. https://doi.org/10.2307/365104.

CT Digital Archive. "Southington Directory for 1876." Accessed April 18, 2024. https://ctda-dev1-lib.grove.ad.uconn.edu/node/7483.

Dolan, J.R. *The Yankee Peddlers of Early America.* New York: C.N. Potter, 1964. http://archive.org/details/yankeepeddlersof00dola.

Evening Post. April 30, 1842. Accessed March 1, 2024. https://www.newspapers.com/image/32114810.

Gall, Henry R., and William George Jordan. *One Hundred Years of Fire Insurance— Being a History of the Aetna Insurance Company Hartford, Connecticut, 1819–1919.* Redditch, Worcestershire, UK: Read Books Ltd., 2017.

Goddard, Stephen B. *Colonel Albert Pope and His American Dream Machines: The Life and Times of a Bicycle Tycoon Turned Automotive Pioneer.* Jefferson, NC: McFarland & Company, 2015.

Green, Constance McLaughlin. *Eli Whitney and the Birth of American Technology.* Boston: Little, Brown, 1956.

Hartford Courant. "Amon Bradley Announces Radical Alterations at the Bradley House." September 1, 1897.

———. "The Bradley Memorial Chapel, Southington." May 29, 1908.

———. December 8, 1911. Accessed March 1, 2024. https://www.newspapers.com/image/369334803.

———. February 25, 1973. Accessed March 7, 2024. https://www.newspapers.com/image/372474638.

———. June 8, 1907. Accessed March 1, 2024. https://www.newspapers.com/image/369471422.

———. June 14, 1965. Accessed April 29, 2024. https://www.newspapers.com/image/370955222.

———. March 9, 1911. Accessed March 2, 2024. https://www.newspapers.com/image/369387413.

———. May 7, 1863. Accessed April 22, 2024. https://www.newspapers.com/image/369181725.

———. May 12, 1863. Accessed April 11, 2024. https://www.newspapers.com/image/369182250.

———. October 22, 1906. Accessed March 7, 2024. https://www.newspapers.com/image/369318650.

———. September 1, 1896. Accessed March 2, 2024. https://www.newspapers.com/image/369288233.

Hoppen, K. Theodore. *The Mid-Victorian Generation, 1846–1886.* New York: Oxford University Press, 2000.

Internet Archive. "Pressed Glass in America: Encyclopedia of the First Hundred Years, 1825–1925: Welker, John, 1915." Accessed April 29, 2024. https://archive.org/details/pressedglassinam0000welk/page/n1/mode/2up.

Jaffee, David. *A New Nation of Goods: The Material Culture of Early America.* Philadelphia: University of Pennsylvania Press, 2010.

Jerome, Chauncey. *History of the American Clock Business for the Past Sixty Years and Life of Chauncey Jerome.* New Haven, CT: Read Books Ltd., 2017.

Journal. December 11, 1903. Accessed February 23, 2024. https://www.newspapers.com/image/675146475.

———. March 5, 1907. Accessed March 11, 2024. https://www.newspapers.com/image/675237720.

———. November 3, 1922. Accessed March 8, 2024. https://www.newspapers.com/image/675915611.

———. October 10, 1898. Accessed March 27, 2024. https://www.newspapers.com/image/675093030.

Le Blanc, Paul. *A Short History of the U.S. Working Class: From Colonial Times to the Twenty-First Century.* Chicago, IL: Haymarket Books, 2017.

Marquis, Albert Nelson, ed. *Who's Who in New England.* N.p.: A.N. Marquis, 1909.

National Endowment for the Humanities. "Litchfield Enquirer. [Volume] (Litchfield, Conn.) 1829–Current, April 14, 1864, Image 1." April 14, 1864. https://chroniclingamerica.loc.gov/lccn/sn84020071/1864-04-14/ed-1/seq-1.

———. "Litchfield Enquirer. [Volume] (Litchfield, Conn.) 1829–Current, January 21, 1847, Image 2." January 21, 1847. https://chroniclingamerica.loc.gov/lccn/sn84020071/1847-01-21/ed-1/seq-2.

———. "The New Haven Union (New Haven, Conn.), 1895–192?, December 18, 1913, CITY EDITION, Image 10." December 18, 1913.

Princeton Institute for Historic Research. *Automobile Quarterly* (1962). http://archive.org/details/automobilequarte44janprin.

Rainer, Joseph T. "The 'Sharper' Image: Yankee Peddlers, Southern Consumers, and the Market Revolution." *Business and Economic History* 26, no. 1 (1997): 27–44. http://www.jstor.org/stable/23703298.

Record-Journal. February 2, 1980. Accessed April 15, 2024. https://www.newspapers.com/image/675903339.

———. March 5, 1907. Accessed February 24, 2024. https://www.newspapers.com/image/675305216.

Schäfer, Stefanie. "The Yankee Peddler Conjures an American Marketplace." In *Yankee Yarns: Storytelling and the Invention of the National Body in Nineteenth-Century American Culture*. Edinburgh, SCT: Edinburgh University Press, 2021. https://www.jstor.org/stable/10.3366/j.ctv1vtz8bk.8.

Slap, Andrew L., and Michael Thomas Smith. *This Distracted and Anarchical People: New Answers for Old Questions about the Civil War–Era North*. Bronx, NY: Fordham University Press, 2013. http://ebookcentral.proquest.com/lib/salve-ebooks/detail.action?docID=3239784.

State of Connecticut. *Private and Special Laws of the State of Connecticut*. 1837. Hartford: Connecticut State Library, Connecticut Historical Society.

———. *The Public Records of the Colony of Connecticut* [1636–1776]…: *1757–1762*. Press of the Case, 1880.

Timlow, Herman R. *Ecclesiastical and Other Sketches*. N.p.: Books on Demand, 2023.

Tioga Eagle. June 12, 1850. Accessed February 26, 2024. https://www.newspapers.com/image/37127690.

Trumbull, James Hammond. *The Memorial History of Hartford County, Connecticut, 1633–1884*. Hartford, CT: E.L. Osgood, 1886.

U.S. Census, 1880. "Francis Dyer." 73a (roll 99). National Archives and Records Administration, 1880. https://www.ancestry.com/discoveryui-content/view/16928420:6742.

Upson Family Association of America. *The Upson Family in America*. Tuttle, Morehouse & Taylor Company, 1940.

Yale University, Class of 1864. *History*. New Haven, CT: C.S. Robinson & Company, printers, 1895.

Yale University, Class of 1864, and Charles Greene Rockwood. *Supplement to the History of the Class of 1864: Yale College (Published in 1895)*. Princeton, NJ: Princeton University Press, 1907.

ABOUT THE AUTHOR

C hristina Volpe, a lifelong resident of Southington, is a historian and curator specializing in Connecticut's Gilded Age and the Second Industrial Revolution. With a focus on New England's industrial history, Christina's expertise is rooted in her academic background, including degrees in archaeology and the classics from the American University of Rome and an MA in public history from Central Connecticut State University. Her career includes roles as an assistant curator and archivist for prominent family archives; she has contributed to institutions such as the Wadsworth Atheneum and, since 2021, has served as curator of the Barnes Museum. Christina serves on several boards, including for the New England Chapter of the Society of Architectural Historians and the *Connecticut History Review Journal*. She is pursuing a PhD in humanities from Salve Regina University ('26).

Visit us at
www.historypress.com